Specimen Angling
By Design

John Searl

SPECIMEN ANGLING BY DESIGN

Martin Hooper

The Crowood Press

First published in 1993 by
The Crowood Press Ltd
Ramsbury, Marlborough
Wiltshire SN8 2HR

British Library Cataloguing in
Publication Data
A catalogue record for this book is available
from the British Library.

ISBN 1 85223 734 1

Picture Credits

A special thank you to Paul Whittal for allowing me to use his photograph of my 3lb 12oz
record grayling, and to Mick Toomer for
obtaining it for me; John Medlow for his pictures of chub and roach; Mark Vials for his
tench pictures; Terry Lampard for the photo
of Tim Norman with Fork in the Tail at its first
time of capture; and Ray Clark with his British
record roach. Thank you to Martin Elliott for
the superb illustrations through the book and
to John Searl for the pencil drawings on pages
2 and 176.

**Typeset and designed by
D & N Publishing
DTP & Editorial Services**
The Old Surgery
Crowle Road
Lambourn
Berkshire RG16 7NR

Phototypeset by FIDO Imagesetting,
Witney, Oxon
Printed and bound in Great Britain by
BPCC Hazells Ltd
Member of BPCC Ltd

Dedication
To Debbie, Kelly and Janine.

I have had the idea of writing a book for some
time, but have not actually got round to it
because of a lack of both time and motivation.
The only occasion I can draw myself away
from water for any long period is during the
closed season; but even then it is difficult to
keep away entirely, what with baiting up
before the season starts, fish spotting and occasionally attempting to cast a fly.

It was my wife Debbie who encouraged and
enabled me to write this book. She makes
most of my baits, cooks the hempseed for me,
posts all my letters, acts as a secretary and still
manages to cope with the two kids. All this
adds up to more time on the bank for me, and
as Debbie also decorated this year during the
closed season, I could get on with my writing.
Not only has my wife done all this, but before
our second daughter Janine was born in July
1991 she allowed me to go fishing as much as
I liked, so long as I took a pager to signal when
the baby was due! I caught three roach the
afternoon that Janine was born, all over 2lb
with the best at 2lb 12oz – and I was there an
hour before the birth, that evening!

Acknowledgements
Not many anglers can say that they have such
wonderful support and I thank Debbie for all
her efforts in every way.

I must also thank Ted Waterman of Ringwood Tackle for all the help he has given me
over the years, Peter Drennan for inventing
the Drennan Cup Competition without which
I would still be an unknown angler, Martin
Kowal of Specialist Bait Supplies, Steve Jones
of North Western Rods, Alan Bramley of Partridge Hooks and Dave Chilton of Kryston
Products.

Contributors
Thanks are also due to Richard Graham for his
account of the 14lb barbel, Mick Bowles for his
account of the 8lb eel (and the photograph),
and all those who have become friends along
the way.

Contents

1

Introduction

This book is written for anyone who aspires to catch large fish consistently, and is aimed specifically at those anglers who are prepared to put a lot of time into their sport so that they can catch the fish they seek. Indeed, a vast amount of my time is spent in locating fish – walking banks and climbing trees in order to spot and observe them – rather than actually getting a baited hook into the water. I probably spend around about 90 per cent of my angling time on rivers in the summer months looking for fish, and only 10 per cent actively fishing.

The waters where I do the majority of my fishing are bright and clear, and so spotting and observing fish behaviour is of paramount importance to me. In other areas, the water may not be so clear, and then you must rely solely on watercraft. In times of flood, which is often the best part of the winter, I am restricted to this method of location myself. However, as I can see the fish at all other times it is far easier for me to locate the larger fish when the water is clear. The fish are not likely to be too far from their normal holding areas, and will probably be in the nearest slacker water above or below their usual haunts, or in a depression in the bed of the river. If the river is only coloured by recent rain and the flow has not greatly increased, the chances are the larger fish will not have moved at all. Obviously, it is a different story with lakes, as it involves mostly watercraft with very little spotting, although fish will on occasion show themselves by rolling.

This book is not an intended as an idiot's guide showing you where to catch fish, nor is it intended to tell you that if you fish using these methods you will catch the biggest fish in the river or lake. No one can emulate completely the methods of another angler, but they can modify such information to suit their own purposes. It is written merely to show the way that I fish, and to tell you about the fish that I have caught, along with the good fish caught by other anglers who use similar methods.

Necessary Investments

When embarking on a campaign in search of better than average fish, certain items are required. They include, first and foremost, a good pair of polarizing fish-spotting glasses. The many hours spent wandering along the banks of rivers and, occasionally, lakes looking for fish are made that much easier if the strain can be taken from the eyes.

Warm and waterproof clothing such as a good-quality wax jacket is worth every penny. The spacious pockets will carry most items required for adopting a mobile approach when tackling rivers, and it will also keep you warm and dry. There is little point in spending hours on the bank localizing a good fish, only to be forced to leave because of a sudden downpour. A one-piece suit is also a good investment for very cold weather and when embarking on long campaigns towards the end of the season.

A good pair of sturdy boots is essential. Personally, I have gone through a number of different types and have finally settled on the Bridgedale Dry Boots – they are light, comfortable, 100 per cent waterproof and ideal for most situations. The exception is in extremely cold weather when I find that Skeetex are useful – there is nothing worse than cold feet! If you intend to go wading, then most brands are suitable. I do not go wading any more unless I have to get a fish out of a weed-bed or something, and then I just jump in anyway providing that the water is not too deep or the weed too dense.

You will need an accurate set of scales for when you do catch that elusive leviathan – Avons are preferable for most species as the dial scale is easy to read and very reliable, and they do not take up too much room. A larger set of scales can be kept in your vehicle should you be fortunate to catch a fish in excess of 40lb. You will also need a weigh sling of industrial nylon, and a good sized keep sack of the same material as it is far kinder to fish than a keep net and is also a lot easier to carry. Remember to buy a good unhooking mat for those 'hard on fish' gravel pits. There are a number of companies producing these, and most good tackle shops stock a variety of choice to suit different species.

Buy a reliable camera, preferably a single lens reflex. The all-automatic self-focusing cameras are very useful, especially if you are on your own. You will need either a tripod or a screw-in adaptor to convert a bank stick to monopod, a long bob, and a flashgun and spare films. Spare batteries are a must; after all, you are likely to be on your own and it would be disastrous if the camera or the flashgun refuses to work through a lack of batteries. If you attempt to buy a camera battery after specialized camera shops have closed, you may well pay far more than the usual prices (see the account of my personal best roach on page 119) or, worse still, you may end up with no photographs at all.

A light, low chair for most normal work and a bed chair for those long sessions at lakes and pits are required. If you are going to do a lot of long session fishing then it is worth investing in a bed chair from the range produced by Fox International. I spent many an uncomfortable night on cheap sun loungers before I got one of their bed chairs, and I consider it worth every penny. A good quality bivvy is also essential, and again Fox have the best – they are easy to put up and have none of the restrictions that the traditional umbrella and over wrap has.

A warm sleeping bag is another must. Again, Fox have the best available. It is amazing just how cold some summer nights can get, never mind the winter ones. Then there is cooking gear if the take-aways are too far, a radio, a colour television, fitted carpets and bivvy slippers, a cool drinks dispenser, an electric blanket, spare chairs for guests . . .!

Membership of fishing clubs and, if you get into any of them, syndicate waters are of far more use for general angling than buying day tickets on a regular basis. Certainly, such membership will offer much better value for money. The restrictions to fishing are usually far less and a lot of clubs offer access in the coarse fishing closed season to trout or salmon fishing waters. This will give you a valuable insight into fish behaviour and movements prior to 16 June, and, if you are so inclined, it will give you a chance to cast the odd fly or spinner around for trout and salmon as well.

Tackle

Hooks

Without exception, the most important item of tackle is the hook. You may have all the right gear, but if you have a bad hook on the end of it then no amount of brilliant playing will stop your fish from getting off should it decide to bury itself in a weed-bed. The hook has to be suitable for the species of fish you are trying to catch. The range of specialist hooks made by such companies as Peter Drennan International and Partridge of Redditch will provide all the hooks you should ever need. The introduction of chemically sharpened hooks has meant that the sharpening stone has become almost obsolete. However, always check this type of hook after catching a fish and particularly if you have dragged it out of a snag, weed-bed or other obstruction. The points, although brilliantly sharp to start with, do not have very good abrasion resistance and are prone to turning over at the extreme point, sometimes even breaking off.

Line
Mainline is very important. I use Maxima for most river fishing and Sylcast for pike, eel, tench and carp fishing, but this is very much a personal choice. The material that I use most for hook lengths is Kryston – indeed, I very rarely use monofilament these days except when float fishing or when livebaiting for perch – and, of course, wire when pike, zander or eel fishing. In the season before writing this book I experimented with Kryston for eels, but as I had an estimated 8lb eel shred my trace at the net on the opening night, I would not recommend it!

A recent introduction to my tackle box has been the wire-coated Kevlar marketed by Neville Fickling. It is far more supple than normal wire and presentation is obviously better than standard wire. However, it does have a tendency to slip under pressure and far more care is needed to make reliable traces – superglue on the turns goes some way to alleviating this problem.

Rods
I have a number of rods for coarse fishing, including two 12ft, 2¼lb test, through-action general rods; two 1¾lb test, through-action tench/zander rods; two 1¼lb test, through-action general rods; two quivertip rods, mostly for roach and chub fishing; a 14ft float rod for trotting; and a 13ft spliced-in-tip float rod for catching bait and for dace fishing. Specialist companies such as Graham Phillips rods, Drennan International and Shimano will provide a good selection of rods for the specialist angler.

Reels
If you can find them, buy centre pins for most river fishing and fixed spools for lakes. Modern pins such as the Swallow Pin (although this is not a true pin in the sense of the word as it runs on bearings rather than on the pin itself) are priced well and work adequately. Aerial, Speedias and Trudex are some of the better original pins, but a good one costs money. Gone are the days when you could pick up an old pin at a car boot sale for next to nothing.

A new pin has recently come on to the market called the Trophy Reel. This reel is somewhat different in its construction to other pins in that it is machined from high-quality solid aluminium. Again, this is not a true pin as it runs on ball races. It is fitted with a rubber 'O' ring to the outside edge of the pin. I found that it took some getting used to as it was a new concept, and at first I did not feel happy with it. However, the reel does afford good grip in adverse conditions, it certainly helps when batting the reel and it is a lot easier on the fingers.

I am not a lover of fixed spools, but when fishing on lakes the fixed spool is far more versatile than the pin. I have four Shimano Baitrunners which I use for pike, carp, tench, zander and eel fishing. I would, however, use a pin for piking on rivers if I had one suitable, the Grice and Young Big Piker being the obvious choices. Eel fishing always demands a fixed spool – as will be evident later. I have also recently invested in two more small Shimanos for lake roaching and for use when free-line fishing.

A selection of the author's centre pins. Centre: a Trudex. Clockwise from the top: a modified Speedia, a three-ratchet Speedia, a Fred Crouch Aerial copy, the new Sundridge pin, an Aerial proper and a Dave Swallow centre pin.

Landing Nets
The range of nets marketed under the brand name of Fastnet are excellent, being both light and virtually unbreakable. They are easy to transport whilst moving between swims as they are in one piece with no separate spreader block to lose, and they come with their own carrying bag. There is a choice of sizes of both frame and mesh that will cover most of the fish you wish to catch. Although far more expensive than conventional nets, the only things ever likely to need replacing are the mesh or front cord. The only time when the Fastnet is unsuitable is when eel fishing – for this I use an E. T. large net. The need to get eels as near to the top of the nest as possible before lifting is the reason that the Fastnet is not suitable. The locking mechanism may well foul the line, and if this should happen then the eel is likely to be lost.

Essential Extras
These include bite indicators such as drop-off indicators and monkey climbers, Optonics, Fox or Viper heads, plus buzzer bars and rod pods for hard gravel pits and bank sticks. Various bait droppers, feeders, swivels, rig tube and bins, forceps and disgorgers complete your tackle. Finally, there must be something to put it all in. By far the best item for this is a rucksack. Any camping shop has a good stock of these, but they do tend to be a bit too colourful. The best bet is an ex-Army rucksack, but if you cannot find one then buy a purpose-built rucksack by a company like Wychwood. An angler's quiver by the same company is very useful for the bivvy and bank sticks.

This section may well look like a tackle brochure, but I have only mentioned good-quality products which I use myself. As with everything, tackle is down to personal choice and, in some respects, available funds. Bear in mind though that a cheap product will often be inferior and may well let you down at just the wrong moment!

Pre-Season Preparations

Bait Preparation

The humble earthworm (or lobworm as it is known in the trade) is one of the most effective baits for a variety of coarse fish. The reason this bait is not used extensively is that a certain amount of effort is required to collect enough worms for a day's fishing. Worms can be purchased from some tackle shops, but the price is rather prohibitive unless money is no object.

Collecting and Keeping Lobworms

There are a number of ways in which to collect lobs. The easiest way is to get on friendly terms with your local farmer and follow the plough across the field, fighting off the seagulls that are there for the same reason as you. You can also dig for them, but another successful method is to go on a worm hunt!

Worm hunting is best done in the closed season. The first thing to do is to get something suitable to keep the worms in. The most useful thing for this job is a plastic tank, and you can acquire one or two of these at a demolition site for next to nothing. Once you have a tank, drill a couple of dozen holes along the underside of it. Place 4in of fine gravel in the bottom of the tank, place layers of newspaper over this, and then finish off with a mixture of finely sieved soil moss and shredded newspaper. The gravel allows for drainage and prevents a lot of the worms from entering the bottom of the tank and escaping via the drainage holes.

Now, on to the hunting itself. Although worms can be caught on most nights (apart from when the weather is very cold), the time to get the best results is after heavy rainfall when the temperature is reasonably high. Aim to arrive an hour or so after dark. The items you will require are a dim torch, a bucket and a rag of some sort to keep your fingers dry. In light of my own experiences, perhaps you should also prepare a good story for the police when they arrive to see what you are doing . . .

On one particular occasion I was working a golf course in a rather up-market area of Bournemouth when I suddenly became aware of blue flashing lights and officers of the local constabulary running about in all directions. They had apparently received a report of a strange person with a torch crawling around near the boundary overlooking some rather posh houses. As a few burglaries had taken place in the preceding weeks, they thought that I may well have been on the look out for a team of burglars or something more sinister. The bucket of worms, however, seemed to convince them and I was joined by two officers crawling around on their hands and knees for a while collecting worms for me. I often wonder what they told their sergeant when they went off duty that night covered in mud!

Work your way slowly across a grassy area such as a golf course and when you spot a worm grasp it near to the hole and pull it out.

12

The River Frome – an excellent grayling river.

Sometimes the worms will come out of the hole easily and may even already be out of it altogether. If this is the case so much the better, but if it is not then steadily pull the worm from the hole. Once you become familiar with the method, a steady pressure can be maintained until the worm releases its grip on its burrow and slides out without becoming damaged. On a good night hundreds or even thousands of worms can be obtained in this way. Any that you break in the process should be discarded.

On arrival home, spread the worms out on the top of the soil mixture and leave them well alone until morning. Any worms that have not then gone down into the soil must be removed, even if nothing appears wrong with them. As one bad apple spoils the barrel, so the same is true with one bad worm.

In times of dry weather water the soil in your tank well. You cannot overwater it as any excess will drain through the gravel and exit via the holes. Turn the soil frequently with a fork and remove any suspect worms; this also serves to harden the worms up by forcing them to work a lot harder than they would do normally. It is useful to place a few turfs on top of the soil as this will stop it drying out too quickly and also feeds the worms. Every month or so remove half of the soil and replace it with fresh soil to avoid any accumulation of bacteria. Any worms left over from a fishing trip should be treated as if you had just collected them and placed on top of the soil or turf – discard any the following morning if necessary. Often, worms will start to breed in the tank: these will grow on if left and will supplement your supply for the season.

Canned Baits
It is a good idea to stock up on tins of meat and corn before the season starts – the less time spent in supermarket queues during the season the better. There is nothing worse than getting an unexpected after-noon off work and then having to spend half of it in a supermarket waiting to buy a tin of luncheon meat.

Seed Baits
Seed baits such as hemp can be purchased in bulk and prepared in advance for the coming season and for pre-baiting. I prepare all of my seed baits in bulk, 4 gallons at a time. For this purpose I purchased a rigid plastic 5-gallon dustbin, along with a kettle element and lead. I simply drilled a hole in the bottom of the bin and screwed the kettle element in place. Now all I need to do is fill the bin with seeds and water, switch on the power and bring to the boil. By the morning all the seeds have split and are ready for use.

Over the years I have found that hemp that has started to go off a bit is far better than fresh bait. This discovery was made when I found myself running a bit short on fresh hemp – the choice was to stop feeding altogether or to use some that had been festering in my bucket for a few days. As the barbel I had in front of me had started to thin out anyway, I decided to use the disgusting mixture that was in the bucket. I fully expected to kill the swim completely, but to the contrary the bar-bel loved it! Now I try to keep a supply of hemp that is a few days old to use as feed.

Hemp can be frozen ready for use once the season starts if you have access to a freezer. If you do not, then prepare the hemp around a week before the season starts so that it has begun to go off. As soon as one bucket is started, cook another so that you can use it in rotation. This method seems to work with all seed baits and not just hemp. Do not leave the seed too long, however, as rancid bait that has gone too far will have an adverse effect!

Tackle Preparation

All line from reels should be stripped and replaced just before the start of the season. Make any repairs to rods, paying particular attention to ring seats. Landing net mesh, and weighing slings and sacks should be checked for damage at the end of the season, washed and dried, and replaced if necessary. It is a good idea to go through all your bait containers at the end of the season and wash the lot out. Leave the lids off once this is done. Batteries must also be removed from electronic bite alarms at the end of the season, or you could find yourself paying out vast amounts of money to replace them.

Pre-baiting

The most important pre-season preparation is to get out there and do some fish spotting. The fish during the closed season are easy to find, especially during spawning time. Chub and barbel can be found on the shallow gravel runs, pike and perch in the entrances to feeder streams or shallow areas of lakes and rivers, and every other fish you care to mention will show itself without taking too much notice of you. The exceptions to this rule are eels. If they are spawning, the cost of getting to the Sargasso Sea is a bit prohibitive! No one has yet seen eels spawn owing to the depths at which this is presumed to take place.

If clubs allow the practice, then start pre-baiting the swim for your chosen species a couple of weeks before the season starts. This includes putting a small section of deadbaits in for eels, but obviously not amongst your other baits.

2

Eels

I suppose everyone has a favourite fish with which to start the season. For most this is probably the tench or carp, but for me it is the eel, with tench running almost alongside! For most nights during the first week or so I will have eel rigs out in the hours of darkness, switching back to tench at first light. As tench do not feed until around dawn, the hours of actual darkness can be spent more effectively fishing for eels. In my case, if good eels are on the feed then tench fishing may well take a back seat on some early morning spells. To most, eels are a strange choice, but there is something that has drawn me to start most years now with eels in mind. It all started in 1987.

Simon Ellis, Dave Tissington and I had all been on a stretch of the River Stour for most of the day. It was one of those days when nothing had gone right. The sun was up and blazing, far too bright it seemed for the chub and barbel we were seeking. After some discussion we decided that the best thing for the night would be eel fishing. It was a somewhat hasty affair. First, to enable us to collect a few small fish for bait, one of us had to get the maggots – Dave was elected. With nothing suitable to keep livebait in, I was delegated to get a bucket and air pump from home, while Simon was given the most important job of being sent on the beer run!

We all arrived at the lake after achieving these tasks within minutes of one another. A few baits were caught quickly, and with an hour or so to kill before dark we started to consume the beer. Having drunk the lot, we decided to get some more – Simon organized a whip-round for funds and came back with quite a few cans of lager. We all set up and cast our baits out, placing the rods on Optonics and arranging our sleeping bags in a row on the bank. We were at the narrow end of the lake where the only fishable swim, if you could call it that, was in the middle. I cast to the right, Dave straight in front and Simon to the left so that we had this end of the lake covered with six fresh deads. Each one of us had one bait on the first drop off and another cast into the deep water, and when I say deep I mean it – the second drop went down to 25ft, and this was only 12yd out.

We consumed the rest of the beer and by midnight were all fast asleep. I was awakened by a screaming Optonic and looked up at the same time as Dave. Simon's far rod had line peeling from it at an alarming rate. And Simon? He slept on. Not one to shy away from opportunities such as this, I leapt (or, more truthfully, staggered!) from

A 3lb eel caught amidst the flowers.

my sleeping bag and struck for him. The strike met with nothing, and after reeling in the bait was inspected. There was no apparent damage and I recast.

I had just got back into my sleeping bag when the same Optonic screeched yet again. I looked at Dave and we both looked at Simon – there was not a sign of life. Drastic action being required, I woke him with a swift poke in the ribs, using a large stick that was lying near me. I was not going to keep on looking after his rods for him! He crawled sloth-like toward his rods, picked the offending rod from the rests and closed the bail arm.

All of us, and in particular Simon, suddenly realized that this was no run-of-the-mill eel. Before he had a chance to pull the hook home, the rod was pulled right over. Now, we all fish with the clutch as tight as we can get it. The reasoning behind this is that if an eel is allowed to take line it is more likely to make it to the snags, and if it can spin the clutch then this is even more likely. Well, this eel managed to spin the clutch anyway – not fast, just a steady slip of around a yard at a time. Simon clamped down with one hand, and then leaned into the fish and managed to gain about three or four yards by pumping the rod. Feeling as if he had now regained control, he made the obvious statement that this was a good fish. The eel, however, decided to show

The author with a 5lb 2oz eel.

who was boss and took off on another run, taking more line than Simon had gained. This toing and froing continued for some five minutes or so, with the rod tip at times pointing directly at the fish and Simon trying to keep it from the snags.

Simon is not a weak man, and to be honest I was amazed at the power this fish had. The final run really had to be seen to be believed, the fish taking off with Simon desperately trying to stop the clutch from spinning. It was a valiant effort to prevent it from reaching the snags, but the fish made it.

With the fish now firmly in the snags the inevitable happened. After more pulling with some nasty grating noises emitting from the line, it finally snapped with a sound like a rifle shot in the otherwise quiet night. After some discussion we decided that the fish had got too far out in the first place owing to Simon's slow reaction to the initial run. The line was checked for damage and Simon removed a few yards that were badly frayed. After tackling back up again, he cast the bait roughly to the same spot. The rod had only been on the rest for two minutes at the most when a blistering run signalled another take. This time Simon was on it before it had gone three yards. The resulting fight was much the same, with the eel demolishing the tackle and Simon in the process. An inspection of the rod in the morning revealed that the rings had a number of grooves caused by the friction of the line, and for the record, none of us could turn the clutch on Simon's reel by hand! Oh, another thing! Simon's stomach and arm muscles ached for quite a while!

And as for Dave and I? We had one run between us – on my nearest rod – which turned out to be a tench of around 2lb. Yes, other fish do take roach heads, including roach! Well, that is the reason that the two others and I were often at this lake for the first night of the season, and for a few other nights as well. Between us, however, we have had little success on this water. The largest eel was one of 4lb 3oz – a good fish, but not of the calibre that the water undoubtedly holds. No one has hooked one of the large eels again, and the largest eel to come from this water that we have heard of was a fish of over 7lb. This eel was taken, I am led to believe, on maggot in the middle of the day in October. It is only a rumour and as yet has not been substantiated, although I tend to think that there is some truth in it. Unfortunately for us, however, the lake has now been taken over by a club and night fishing is not allowed!

So that is how I got hooked on eels. I had caught eels before and my best then stood at 4lb 14oz, a fish that had not put in a very good account of itself. I had never considered eels a worthy fish until that day, and now I spend a great deal of my time during the summer months pursuing them.

Techniques and Tactics

The most important thing you need to know about eel fishing is that the slightest resistance is likely to result in a dropped run. This is not the case with average eels of around 2lb or below as they do not seem to care too much what you do, but refers to the larger eels which may accept your offerings – it is doubtful that you will hook one of these should it feel any resistance.

With this in mind, you have to arrange for bite indication to be resistance free with the line being able to exit the reel without causing any undue friction. Obviously, the reel for the job has to be a fixed-spool type. It also needs to have a good lay of line in order to eliminate bedding in. The bale arm has to be left open with the line stopped from peeling from the lip of the spool unless a fish has taken the bait. There are various methods of achieving this, but by far the simplest two methods are as follows.

The first is the 'penny on the top of the spool' method. This dates from a time before the free-running electronic bite alarms were invented. The audible side of the alarm was provided by a suitable hub-cap, Ford Cortina Mark II hub-caps being the best – whether this was because they were readily available courtesy of kerbside motors, I am not quite sure! The fish pick up the bait and move off, thereby causing the penny to drop into the hub-cap and alerting the angler to a run. This method has its drawbacks, however, as on windy nights the movement of the line is likely to cause many false alarms, and most Ford Cortinas these days have already been relieved of their hub-caps!

The second method, and the one I prefer, is to position a short needle with a very light monkey climber at an angle of approximately 45 degrees so that the top of the needle is a couple of inches under and behind the open spool of the reel. This allows the eel to pick up the bait and move off with the minimum amount of resistance. The number of false alarms is greatly reduced and, of course, the weight of the monkey can be varied to suit the conditions, keeping it as light as possible.

Eels provide a worthy opponent for any angler both in the way they fight, as illustrated earlier, and in that they are not the easiest of fish to catch. I accept that the small ones are a right pain and that you can catch them all the time, especially when not fishing for them, but larger specimens do not do the things associated with these easier-to-catch and often hated 'bootlaces'. Large eels fight extremely hard, but once on the bank often behave rather well – they do not, however, appear to respect your wishes for a decent photograph and will often prove extremely difficult to hold.

The J. S. Rig

The best all-time resistance-free rig must be the one invented by the late John Sidley, the J. S. rig. For bottom fishing it has no competition. The rig allows for almost tangle-free casting every time, providing that the line is feathered prior to its entry into the water – this causes the rig to straighten out. You can fish with confidence when using this rig, knowing that if an eel picks up the bait it can do so cleanly 99.9 per cent of the time. With bites on some waters being very hard to come by, this is of paramount importance. It is soul-destroying if your first run after many hours or nights of waiting results in failure as the bait is dropped because the rig becomes tangled.

The second advantage of the J. S. rig is that no matter how far the bait is from the bank, or which way the eel makes off with it, a run is signalled by the Optonic. It does have one disadvantage, however, in that should the eel run toward you it is possible that you can miss the fish on the strike. In my early years of eel fishing I used to fish with free-lined baits. This is fine so long as the eel does the right thing and moves off with the bait away from the rod. Should it move toward you, however, the most you can hope for is the odd bleep or two. I have spent many a night before I started using the J. S. rig where the bait was taken in toward the bank. If this happens, the eel can remove the bait deftly from the hook without you realizing it until the next morning. How they can actually achieve this is beyond me, but it has occurred. With large eels so hard to come by, this may well have cost me a personal best.

I joined the British Eel Anglers' Club some years ago and the help I received from John was invaluable. All anglers will miss John not only for his dedication to the sport and his tireless efforts in eel conservation, but also for his innovative efforts to solve anglers' problems, and as a man who would help and give advice to anyone who cared to ask. He was a great pioneer who will sadly be missed by all.

The J. S. rig works as well with worm as it does with deadbait, and has another advantage in that it makes light work of dealing with awkwardly hooked fish. In these cases, the hook length can be removed and the fish placed in a sack overnight to be dealt with the following morning. The replacement of the damaged hook length takes a matter of seconds. With this rig, the standard 2oz lead can be changed to a heavy swimfeeder, either with an open or block end. By using a swimfeeder you will be able to push bits of worm, fish or an attractor soaked in cotton wool into it and cast to distances that loose feeding would not allow. As you can see this is a most versatile rig.

A lot of eels are now caught by anglers who fish well off the bottom. The J. S. rig can also be used for this method, but with a few minor adjustments – the use of a larger polyball and a length of stiff tubing to keep the bait away from the line between the polyball and anchor weight. When used in this manner the odd tangle does, unfortunately, occur. Another method is to use the rig as before, but to inject air into the bait to get it off the bottom. This works all right with worms or whole coarse baits, but it is not successful when you use section fish baits or sea baits. In the latter situations, the use of a small polyball tied from the eye of the hook and light breaking strain monofilament seems to work, although dropped runs do still occur.

Eels are split into two main groups: small-mouthed eels, mostly associated with worm fishing as it is thought that these fish are small crustacean feeders; and broad-headed eels with wide, almost semicircular mouths – these are the predators, almost exclusively feeding on fish, both live and dead. There are also eels that are neither one nor the other.

The shape of an eel's head is determined by the type of food it eats, so it stands to reason that if the water you intend to fish is overrun with small, bait-sized fish, then the main population is likely to be the broad-headed (large-mouthed) variety. If, on the other hand, small fish are scarce but the water is rich in crustaceans, then the eels are more likely to be small mouthed.

It is presumed that the small-mouthed variety is the largest of the two main types of eel. This is backed purely by the present British and world record eel of 11lb 2oz, which is a small-mouthed eel (*Anguilla anguilla*). In an article I wrote for *Coarse Fisherman*, I said that a record fish may possibly disprove this theory; since the article was written, one of the British Eel Anglers' Club members has taken a double-figure broad-headed eel. It was taken by Gary Mason, and this has proved that any eel, be it wide or small mouthed, is capable of attaining 10lb or more in weight.

Gary achieved the ambition of all serious eel anglers by catching the second largest fish in history, an eel of 10lb 7oz. This is the first time that an exceptional eel has been caught by someone who was specifically fishing for eels. It was taken on a deadbait and pushed the long-standing Eel Anglers' Club record – held by our illustrious secretary Mick 'Eeling Executive' Bowles – firmly off the top of the list. Not to be completely beaten, Mick has now insisted that he still holds the record for an eel caught at a fish-in! He has also insisted that I include the account of the capture of that fish in this book, so under threat of Mr N Asty and a scandal I agreed; after all, an 8lb eel is rather a good fish anyway. Here follows Mick's own account, some of which is not strictly true as I made a few additions – I will leave it up to you to decide which bits these were!

Mick Bowles' Account of His Eight-Pounder

Finding a suitable water in which large eels actually live is half the battle for any budding eel angler. I was full of anticipation that I may have found such a water when the British Eel Anglers' Club obtained permission from the then owner, Mr Colin Simpson, to try for eels at a trout water, Weirwood Reservoir in Sussex.

As I looked at the water before fishing it, I discovered that the reservoir had been made by damming the upper reaches of the River Medway – this had taken place some thirty-two years earlier. The only exit from the reservoir apart from some small feeder streams entering the water) was via the overflow at the dam wall. The reservoir had all the indications that it held eels, and large ones at that. This seemed especially likely as it held a gigantic coarse fish population.

Further enquiries were not too helpful. The water authority had no records of any eels being found in the water and, according to them, the two species which did not appear to exist in the reservoir were pike and eels. However, on speaking to the water authority workers at the pumping station, I was told that in the fifteen years that they had been working there they had in fact seen two eels in the course of electrofishing. Both of these had been in an area towards the far end of the reservoir on the south bank. One was described as being as thick as a moped tyre, the other more like a motorbike tyre. For me this was enough to be sure that the water contained eels.

When the weekend of the club trip arrived, I was rather disappointed by the turn-out; only two other members had bothered to make the effort. The reason for this was probably due to the stringent

Mick Bowles with his monster.

restrictions and the extortionate fee of £8 per night (this was in case we caught any of the trout). One of the lads decided to fish the south bank from a point, while the other member and I, since we were unable to use boats to get where we had originally wanted to go, chose to fish on the north bank near the dam wall. As it was, we had to climb the wall on the east bank of the dam with all our gear in order to get there, and by the time we reached the top of the wall we were both shattered.

I was further alarmed when I noticed a concrete slipway heading in to the reservoir from the corner of the dam wall. That put paid to my intentions of fishing the corner, as somehow the thought of fishing on a concrete bottom did not inspire much confidence. I walked along the bank a bit further and noticed a lot of small fish in the margins. This seemed as good a place as any, and as I did not feel like walking any further, I dumped my gear. The area I had decided upon gave me the chance to cast toward the dam wall, yet be a distance from it.

The wind was heading down the water straight at the dam. A number of dead fish, including some roach in excess of 2lb, were being washed against the wall (these were probably spawning victims) and the local crow population was helping itself to the spoils. I set my gear up and cast two baits along the edge of the dam wall, and two baits straight out in front of me not far from the margins. In both cases one rod was on worm and the other on deadbait.

The margins were positively alive with fish, with carp and trout crashing out all over the place. My rods, however, remained quiet until between 1.00 a.m. and 1.30 a.m. when I had two takes on the marginal sardine rod. In classic Mick Bowles' style, I missed them both! At 3.00 a.m. I had a steady run on the margin worm rod, and this one I hooked. I have no idea what it was and it shot about all over the place before shedding the hook in the margins. I now discovered that I had been fishing in 6in of water – it pays to check this sort of thing before fishing!

By this time I had decided that I ought to catch something for my £8, and wound the worm rod in from the dam wall. I baited this with fresh worms and cast out about 25yd where I could see a fair number of carp and some trout in the half-light. I discovered later that this water was about 4ft deep. Being rather fed up by then, I chose to have a walk down the bank to see the other club member fishing near me. I had not gone very far when a run developed, and I ran back to the rod and hit it. The rod buckled over as I made contact, and whatever was on the end made a bee-line out into the reservoir. My immediate thoughts were that it was either a carp or a trout, simply because of the speed of the fish. I gave it some side strain, the fish went to my left and then everything became solid. 'Damn it!', I thought to myself, 'It has gone and weeded me.' So I pumped and heaved as hard as I could and suddenly it all went slack.

Having now presumably lost the fish, my temper flared and I wound in like the devil possessed. Suddenly the rod arched over and I realized that the fish must have been running straight at me. This time the fish was fighting in a straight line, and for the first time I thought that it could have been an eel. It was banging the rod about as it tried to back off away from me once again. I called down to my friend Matt and said, 'I think it's an eel, and blow me it's a monster.' Matt came up and took the net, standing in the shallow margins ready to land it. Two yards from him the fish broke surface. 'It is an eel and blow me, it's a monster!' he exclaimed. Then it was in the net. For some unknown reason, on seeing the net the eel shot straight in like a rocket! Perhaps it thought it was a weed-bed or something, but it was the easiest eel netting I have ever known. Matt ran up the bank with the eel in the net, keeping it well away from the water. We laid the net down and looked at her. She was huge and without a doubt was my personal best eel!

The legendary John Sidley rig had worked once again – three lobs, size two Mustard 92641 beak hook, wire trace and 11lb Syclast line. We immediately placed her on unchecked scales in a wet weigh sling and she went to 7lb 14oz. We decided do it more accurately in the morning. Meanwhile, I made a complete idiot of myself by attempting to do handstands and landing flat on my face; I never was any good at gymnastics!

When dawn arrived I got the other club member to come round with his scales, and we weighed the fish on three sets. Two registered 8lb exactly, and the other 5oz over that. On checking these scales later we found that they weighed 5oz heavy, unfortunately putting some doubt on the weight of the owner's personal best eel! (To save any further embarrassment to this club member I will not add his name!) To say the least, I was ecstatic with delight at catching my new personal best, especially as this was on the first night of fishing a new water. Pleasing or what?

Achieving the fish of a lifetime is a feeling one cannot describe, but to quote an oft-used cliché, I was over the moon. Anyway, once the photographs were finished I took the eel back to the margins. I gave her one more loving look and, much to the horror of some watching trout anglers, I released her. We could see her as she moved slowly away towards the middle of the reservoir. As she passed close to a trout angler who was looking most anxiously into the water, he actually lifted one leg out of it! Soon she had disappeared from view back to her home, but I will never forget her.

Being scavengers and opportunists, the different types of eels will be taken at times on almost any bait you are using. Also, even though the lake that you choose to fish indicates that it holds mainly one of the two characteristic types, the chances are that there will also be a few of the others resident in the water. With less competition from their contemporaries for available food, there is a good chance that these will be bigger than individuals from the larger population. With this in mind, it is therefore worth spending the odd night using baits intended for the least numerous variety of eel. The chances are that a deadbait will still possibly be picked up by the larger small-mouthed eels and, when fishing worm, the wide-mouthed eels will have it anyway, but you may just get a large bonus fish.

As a rule, the best time to fish for eels is during the hours of darkness when there is little or no moon, and when it is warm and overcast. There are undoubtedly exceptions to this, and indeed my personal best eel came from a water that was clear on a night when there was a full moon and not a cloud in the sky. This speculative rule

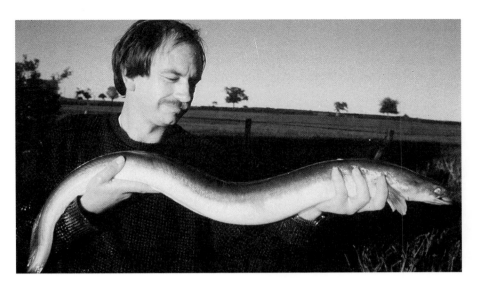

Ken 'Plastic Pig' Jones with his eel.

generally applies to waters that are clear and shallow. Waters that are deep or coloured will produce takes from eels at any time of the day or night, with the eels often showing an inclination to feed from midday through to an hour or so after dark, followed by another main period at first light.

One such water that fits into this latter category is a lake that the British Eel Anglers' Club used for closed season fish-ins. The Severn Trent Water Authority allows eel fishing within its boundaries during the annual closed season, and permission was granted to the club to stage an organized assault on the water in search of eels. With a limited amount of bank space available, places were filled rapidly. Some of the anglers arrived in the middle of the afternoon and set up to fish as soon as they arrived. Others, myself included, took a more leisurely approach and aimed to be on the water about tea-time. This turned out to be a mistake on two counts.

Simon Ellis and I arrived well after 5 p.m., to find that most of the better swims had already been taken. We managed to cram ourselves into a swim in one corner of the lake, and set ourselves up with plenty of time to spare before the expected feeding time at the approach of darkness. Our baits were not even cast out as we thought it a waste of time, and instead we set about arranging the BBQ and winding everyone up with the mouth-watering smell of spit-roasted whole chicken!

Meanwhile, others around us were being plagued with unwanted species – including one or two carp.

Then we heard the shout go up. Ken 'Plastic Pig' Jones was into a large eel. We made our way round to his swim just in time to see it coming up the bank, accompanied by a broadly smiling Mr Jones. As the net was placed on the ground, no one said a great deal. We all knew we were looking at an exceptional fish. Ken removed the hook and duly placed the fish on to the zeroed scales. His face was a picture when the weight of the eel was announced at 6lb 13oz. Every person who was at that fish-in was genuinely pleased for Ken, and anticipation was high for some more eels to follow over the next couple of days. The eels in this water proved to be daylight feeders in the main, and most of the eels caught came during the early morning or evening. Ken's fish was the best taken on the trip and, despite breaking a club rule by turning up in a Reliant Robin, he duly took the club trophy for the best fish!

Eels that live in deeper gravel pits have a tendency to move toward the shallows as night or first light approaches, moving back into the deeper water again as the day goes on.

When fishing with deads there are lots of variables in the way you can present the bait. It can be fished whole or in sections – at times eels will show a preference for either end of a fish or even for the

The author cradles his personal best 6lb 5oz fish.

whole fish. At times livebait will outfish deadbait and at other times using sections will be the only way to get a run. The bait can be placed on the bottom, just under the surface or anywhere in between; the combinations are endless and most frustrating. When fishing deads or worms I tend to fish with one bait off the bottom and one on it.

The way to fish with livebait is to make sure that the bait always attempts to move away from the lead or polyball. The way to achieve this is either to hook the fish in the tail or, if hooked anywhere else in the body or head, to band the fish at the tail root. When using the latter technique, 'the penny on the spool' or monkey climber set at 45 degrees are not suitable methods as the baits will often move enough to cause false alarms. The solution instead is to use a drop-off indicator with an adjustable clip. The clip should be set as light as possible to allow the eel to hit bait out of the clip with the minimum of resistance. If the eel does not get the bait out of the clip on the first time it will almost certainly drop it. Runs from eels are nearly all screamers when using lives, and a short run usually indicates that the bait has pulled out of the clip or that you have a rogue pike. The best rogue pike I have taken was a fish of 23lb 10oz which was caught in the early hours of the morning. It was a most disappointing fish in some respects, as both I and those with me though that it was a very large eel! It was not until it went into the net that we realized that it was in fact a pike.

Bait fish used when eel fishing need to be small. I rarely use anything above a couple of ounces, whether whole livebaits, deads or sections. Deadbaits need to be freshly killed – I have used frozen baits but they tend to be less effective than fresh ones. Collecting livebait can be a simple affair when eel fishing. Small fish will often move into the shallow water near to weed-beds, allowing you to sweep a landing net through the shallows to collect them. You can, of course, catch livebait with a rod and line but this is time consuming and should only be used as a last resort.

The exception to the fresh-killed principle for deadbaits is when using sea-fish baits as it does not seem to matter whether these are freshly killed or frozen. Most sea-fish, and in particular sardines, all have their day whether fished whole or in sections. At certain times of the year, and in particular late summer, sardines will outfish any other type of bait, including fresh-killed coarse fish. This fact was brought to my attention when fishing Broadlands Lake for pike. Using sardine as bait during a rather hot, bright day in October, I experienced a lot of runs that I could not hit. On inspecting the bait when I managed to get it back, I found that there were bits torn out of it right in the middle of the trebles. This is another thing to note about eels – they do seem to know just where to hit a bait with the minimum chance of getting hooked, and thereby making off with a free meal. I never did get an eel out of there, although I actually never fished for them specifically. I regret not taking advantage of the situation as those that did took a number of good eels – the best fish to date over 8lb and taken on sardine!

Whilst eel fishing in Britain is regarded as sport for the slightly mad, this is not really the case. Fair enough, many members of the British Eel Anglers' Club do not appear to be playing with a full deck, but I do not think that this should be taken as a true guide-line! Most anglers I speak to do not see the point of fishing for eels, and feel that they are both a menace and are easy to catch. I can assure you that a large eel is harder to catch than any other type of fish. This is proven by the fact that although double-figure eels turn up in traps all over the country on occasion, they are rarely caught.

In the book *Eels: How to Catch Them* by Raymond Perret there are references to some very large eels. One of these is a fish that was lost at the last moment whilst the author was pike fishing. He compares this particular fish to the size of a small conger of around 15lb. Another found dead in a pond weighed over 11lb, while a third reference is to an eel that was caught in a snag. This latter eel apparently had entangled itself around the snag with stout line – presumably after breaking an angler's tackle. The following day the eel was found dead with a third of its body from the head back missing, and as it still weighed over 8lb the author guesses that its true weight would have been 12lb or more. He goes on to say that if the capture of large eels were pursued with the same concentration as carp fishing then we would get a much better idea of how big eels grow.

Eels, I am afraid, will never get the following that they deserve. A few anglers will, however, continue in the quest for large eels and one day the record may be broken. The odds against this are high purely because of the fact that the large eels do not often make mistakes. If one does, then the chances are that the anglers' bait it has picked up is attached to tackle which is insufficient to deal with it, the result being that it is lost.

Still, as I have said before, there could be a monster lurking in the water near to you – all you have to do is land it.

3

Barbel

Barbel first came to my attention in 1980 when I moved down to Blandford from Manchester. Until then I had not caught one as the rivers around the north-west of England did not contain many resident barbel at the time, apart from the odd illegally stocked fish from the Severn.

It was during a day's chub fishing on the Hampshire Avon that I first hooked a barbel whilst trotting bread. I lost a couple of fish that day which I never saw, and on asking around was told that they had probably been barbel. The next season I set out to catch a barbel specifically, the start of a long campaign to the near exclusion of all other species. I hooked a large number of barbel but lost them all, despite upgrading my tackle so that I could deal with these powerful fish. One day, however, an angler offered his advice on how to land the fish. Basically, he said that I should move down below hooked fish instead of trying to pull them upstream from the weed that they invariably got into. It was then painfully obvious to me that I had overlooked the answer to the problems I had been having. The first fish I landed was a barbel which weighed 5lb 8oz – not big by any means, but at least it was a start.

I spent most of the time from then on catching as many barbel as I could – any barbel. Size did not matter as then it was merely a number's game. I caught doubles up to 12lb 12oz, along with lots of eight- and nine-pounders, but thought little of it. It was not for some time that I realized the significance of a double-figure barbel, and then it was only due to a chance meeting with the angler who had given me the advice on how to land them.

I was a bit annoyed, to say the least, that I had not taken photographs of any of these double-figure fish. Indeed, I hardly ever took photos of anything at all in those days. Still, not worried unduly, I thought it would be easy enough to get some more doubles on the bank and record them on film. I continued to fish in the usual way in

A superb 12lb 9oz barbel.

the hope of catching the target weight, but without success. I caught 8lb fish and the odd 9lb, but fish of over 10lb continued to elude me.

I had to put more thought into the way I was fishing and decided that I needed to be more selective in my methods. The way I went about achieving this was to look for individual fish that looked as if they were doubles and cast bait, usually meat, directly at the fish. This had worked in earlier years when I used to search out trout and grayling for the pot, although obviously luncheon meat was not the bait I used then. To a degree the method worked on barbel too, but the fish were spooked far more easily than trout or grayling. This was probably due to the fact that the aforementioned species only ever made one mistake, then invariably received a quick tap on the head before ending up in the pot. Barbel, on the other hand, had seen it all before and knew when they were being fished for.

I found that I had to cast in with the minimum amount of disturbance upstream of the target fish, and then ease the bait down to it. This method worked up to a point, and I did catch one low double. The method was not particularly successful, however, in that it relied upon being able to spot the fish in the first place – not an easy task when the barbel spent the vast majority of their time hiding under weeds or lying

This superb fish topped 11lb by just one ounce.

motionless on the bottom. When the barbel were in feeding mood, of course, spotting was made that much easier. At this time it became apparent to me that people who were using baits fished over a bed of hemp had far more success in catching barbel than I was having. This was often in swims where I had not seen any barbel. Obviously, the hemp was drawing barbel into the baited swims from other areas.

With this fact in mind, I decided to bait every available swim on a relatively underfished (at that time) stretch of the middle Stour. On arrival at the chosen venue, and armed with a large amount of cooked hemp laced with generous helpings of sweetcorn, I was pleased to find only one other angler on the water. I dropped my tackle into a swim in the middle of the fishery that I knew contained a number of barbel. I then proceeded to bait the whole of the stretch, throwing a good handful into every swim where I could see the bottom and working from the top down to the boundary. In all, this covered some 1½ miles of water. I then went back to the top and worked my way down, noting those swims that contained barbel and topping up with bait all those which had fish feeding in them. Whilst I was doing this, the other angler left the fishery so that I had the whole of the stretch to myself. This area is now heavily fished, so the approach I used is somewhat limited there.

One swim in particular held some good fish, including several doubles. The swim that I otherwise would probably have fished only held fish up to a maximum of around 8lb. Needless to say, I was soon on my way to the doubles swim. I spent a great deal of time up a large willow tree that afforded a complete view of the whole swim, continuing to top the swim up with bait at regular intervals. When I say that I topped it up with bait, I really should say that I was piling it in! I ended up with twenty-seven barbel feeding in there, along with chub and some large roach. Over twenty barbel had moved in from the swims below and above to join the original five fish that I had spotted. Whilst watching from my vantage point it became apparent that the group of larger fish – including four doubles – tended to feed towards the back of the swim, apparently unwilling to become involved in the general mêlée for food that their smaller brethren were engaged in.

To capitalize on this fact, I started to introduce a small amount of bait at the lower end of the swim whilst continuing to pile the bait in at the top. This proved to be successful in dividing the fish some distance apart, with the larger fish only being joined occasionally by fish from the main group. Once I felt confident of taking one of the better fish, I cast a bait gently into the lower part of the swim where the big fish were lying along with a couple of smaller fish. One of these smaller fish decided to pick up the bait and proceeded to slam the rod right round. This resulted in an 8lb fish being hustled from the swim and appearing on the bank after a very short time. I expected this to have dispersed the larger fish from the swim, but after putting the eight-pounder back a short distance upstream, I found the others still feeding in the swim. At my second attempt all was looking good when another smaller fish literally took the bait from the nose of one of the doubles. This one was a seven, and it charged all over the swim scattering the main shoal in different directions. The larger fish thinned out and disappeared into the weeds below.

I was sure that this was certain death, but amazingly, upon coming back to the swim after returning this fish upstream, the large fish were once again feeding happily as if nothing had occurred. After recasting, one of the doubles moved up the swim in direct line with my baited hook, taking in mouthfuls of food and gravel (which it ejected after sifting the bait) on its way. Then it was on my bait and it picked it up. The strike made contact, and after a short but impressive fight the fish was safely on the bank and registering 10lb 12oz on my scales. After having its photo taken the barbel was returned, again a short distance upstream. By this time all of the double-figure fish had departed from

The 10lb 12oz barbel.

A heavily built, upper Avon, 10lb 3oz fish.

the swim and did not return during the following few weeks that I spent fishing for them. I caught a lot of fish in that swim, including six fish of 9lb, but not one of the double-figure fish made even a short appearance in the swim, and I did not manage to locate them anywhere along the length of the stretch. However, some time later they did turn up again in this swim and a friend caught the same double that I had taken at a slightly higher weight of 10lb 14oz. The other doubles were with it, but again they disappeared after the first of the group was caught.

From this, I can only come to the conclusion that once a fish is caught from this particular group the rest vacate the area and only return after they have spent a considerable amount of time elsewhere. Perhaps this is one method fish employ to avoid capture.

Barbel Behaviour

Still on the subject of visible waters, you would think it safe to assume that you would be able to spot all of the barbel that a stretch contains. Let us say for argument's sake that the best fish spotted is in the region of 11lb or so. Having decided that this is the best fish that has shown in the swims you have baited and therefore the biggest on the stretch, you start to fish for it. After introducing more bait, let us imagine that a larger fish than the one originally in the swim moves in – say, 13lb or so in weight – and starts feeding with the other barbel. What do you do when the eleven-pounder picks up the bait first? Most anglers would set the hook, being happy with another double to add to his or her list. Personally, however, I would try to avoid the lesser fish in the hope that if it picked up the bait it would then eject it. As I described earlier, previous experiences have shown me that often the capture of the first double-figure fish will severely jeopardize any chance that I may have at the larger fish. On occasions I have regretted this as I have had fish that I have not caught before pick up a bait, only to miss a larger fish later in the day. As a result, I have refused fish of 12lb on more than one occasion whilst after an exceptional fish.

This behaviour does not only occur when barbel see other barbel caught. On one stretch in particular that I have fished, the barbel definitely used the chub as 'markers'. These conclusions are not restricted to myself, but have also been reached by such anglers as Terry Lampard, Richard Graham, Andy Harman, John Medlow and others who fish this stretch of the middle Stour. It got to such a stage that if you caught a chub you would have to move to another swim. On a number of separate occasions and to different anglers, myself included, the first bite of the session produced a barbel. These were fish of 9lb 15oz (Simon Ellis's first fish from here in three years), 12lb 7oz (my first fish from the stretch after seven years), 11lb 10oz (Andy Harman's first barbel after four years) and Richard Graham's 14lb fish – of which more later.

This particular stretch of the Stour has got to rate as one of the hardest in the Wessex area. I have caught more than one barbel in one day from a swim in the stretch during recent years but these have been from a swim that contains a number of small fish as well as up to three doubles. I have only managed to get one of these doubles out so far, and that was an eleven-pounder – again, the first fish out. I did hook this fish once more in the same season when the other doubles were evident in the swim, but did not want it as the others were larger and,

A double is returned to the Dorset Stour.

of course, because it was a recapture. On the occasions when the large fish were in the swim, the capture of anything from that swim saw the departure of these fish for an indefinable period. The smaller barbel, along with the chub and roach, however, did not seem unduly worried about this and appeared to be permanently resident. The larger fish on the other hand, along with the rest of the big fish in this stretch, appeared to be somewhat nomadic. They could often be seen in a certain swim on one day, only to disappear the following day. This even happened if they had not been fished for.

Recently, however, things have changed on this stretch of water. For some unknown reason, some of the larger barbel are no longer spooked by the capture of chub. This became apparent in the season of 1990–1 in one of the other swims when an unwanted chub picked my bait up and hooked itself. Although the barbel moved out of the swim, they soon returned. When this happened again I took advantage of it and hit every chub that picked the bait up. The end result was that within two days the chub became very wary of two grains of corn, as most had by now been hooked, and gave the barbel a chance to get on to the bait. However, the result of pulling my first barbel out, a 10lb 13oz fish, was that the rest left the area. On this occasion they did not completely disperse from the area, but could be seen hiding on the far bank in the swim below the one I was fishing. The following day, I managed to get them to come across and feed under my feet in a small run between two weed-beds. Within two minutes of positioning a bait on the gravel where I could see it, I hooked and landed a barbel of 11lb 15oz. This fish proved to be the same one that Richard Graham had taken at 14lb.

Whilst on the subject of fish movements, it is worth illustrating the distances that an easily identifiable fish – affectionately known as Ten Spot – has covered in one particular season. I first caught this fish around 200yd from the entrance point to a stretch of the River Stour. It was in a group of fish that included three doubles and a couple of nine-pounders. Ten Spot is so named because of a large black spot near the lateral line in front of its dorsal fin. This spot is clearly visible while the fish is still in the water. There is a definite advantage when having an easily identifiable fish in a stretch of water in that it makes the judging of another fish's size that much easier should it be in the same swim. Also, being able to track an easily identifiable fish's movements is simplicity itself.

Ten Spot, easily identified by the large black spot on its side.

The stretch of water in which Ten Spot lives is a fish-spotter's paradise in that for the majority of its 3-mile length the water rarely exceeds 5ft in depth. Just a few days after my first capture of Ten Spot, I saw a good fish under some weed around half a mile downstream. Once I had coaxed it out from under the weed to start feeding on the free offerings, it became clear that this was the same fish and I left the swim. Some weeks later, at the top of the stretch and whilst fishing for two good fish that I had been after for a few days, I saw another barbel lurking in the weeds at the back of the swim. After an hour it was in with the other fish, happily feeding on the hemp and corn; yes, the new arrival was Ten Spot. This gave me a good idea of the size of the other two fish, and confirmed that my original estimates of 11lb and 12lb were correct. Unfortunately, the only bite I had that evening after the light had faded came from Ten Spot – this time weighing 2oz less than when I last caught it. This cost me a chance at the other two fish as, although they had not departed from the swim the following day, they had become wary and proved impossible to catch. Within two days they had disappeared altogether. The approximate distance that Ten Spot had covered in those few weeks was around 2 miles.

The following season Ten Spot showed up again, when a friend of mine had it at 10lb 6oz. This was on another stretch which the barbel would have had to negotiate two cobbled weirs to get to. Some three weeks later it was caught again, this time at the entrance point near to where I had my first encounter with it.

The fact that this particular barbel had moved a total of over 5 miles and back again during two seasons shows that some fish have a very wide territory. Others seem to be happy to stay in the same place for most of the time, but even they are prone to disappearing on odd occasions, perhaps going elsewhere if pressure dictates.

There are known cases of fish being moved either above or below a weir, only to show up again back in the original swim within a very short time. This begs the question as to whether the fish had already found its way through these obstacles before the angler moved it, and had decided that it wanted to stay where it was. Fish that are moved long distances or to new rivers, however, do not know where they are and have to sort out for themselves where they choose to live. Perhaps this is one of the reasons that stockings, whether legal or not, are often unsuccessful in establishing population of fish, as barbel are prone to split up and go their separate ways. If these barbel then do not meet up and spawn, this can mean that isolated pockets of very large fish may sometimes turn up infrequently until they die off.

The most obvious successes of barbel stocking are those which took place in such rivers as the Dorset Stour, originally stocked by Mr Gomm, an angler from London, with 100 Thames barbel from the Staines area. These were transported using horse and cart in September 1893 to Iford Bridge on the Stour. Some of these fish, it is supposed, then worked their way into the Hampshire Avon via Clay Pool. Subsequently, the Avon received its own stockings at various times in parts throughout the river up to Salisbury. Of course, the history of the Avon and, to a lesser extent the Stour, has been well documented over the years, and I therefore see little point in mentioning the various fish, or indeed persons, that have at one time held the British barbel record.

More recently, the Severn was stocked by the *Angling Times* with a consignment of barbel ranging from 2lb to 9lb which I have been informed were obtained from a trout-only section of the River Kennet in 1956. This was not the first stocking of the water, but is generally accepted to be the one from which the present stocks came. The River Ribble and River Dane were soon to follow, stocked originally during the late 1960s with fish solicited from the Severn, plus to a lesser extent the Wensum. In the case of the Wensum, although there are a number of large fish still present, there are only limited amounts of small fish

A super-fit 8lb 15oz barbel. Note the 5-gallon bait bucket!

in evidence. In the season of 1991–2, there have been more small fish introduced and, no doubt, the progress of these will be monitored by anglers in the Norwich area.

Of course, the Wensum – along with other rivers throughout the country – has suffered badly from low water levels in recent years. I have been told on good authority that this has meant that the barbel are concentrated in groups around the vicinity of weirs. While this may lead to more successful spawning, it certainly will not help in the years to come if these low water conditions continue. The rivers mentioned above, having never had indigenous stocks of barbel, have been the most successful cases of stockings, all holding good to fair numbers of fish of all sizes.

Examples of relatively unsuccessful stockings include the Kentish Stour, the River Nene, the Sussex Ouse, the Rother and the Medway. Of these, the most disastrous stockings have been those on the Kentish Stour and the River Nene, with hardly a fish reported. The Medway, whilst producing a fair number of large fish, has very few small fish as a back-up, but at least some small fish are caught and perhaps this river stocking will eventually be classed as a success. The Rother and Ouse do produce the odd fish of a fair size, but very little caught overall. These rivers are only picked out as examples, and I have missed out a lot of rivers that have had fish injected into them with varying results. In all the cases mentioned, the stock fish have come from the Thames or its tributaries, either directly or indirectly.

More fish are being introduced by enterprising clubs throughout Britain as each year passes – both in rivers and in stillwaters. It seems that everyone wants barbel on their doorstep, and if the clubs or water authorities will not play ball then they are helped via the back of an angler's car.

Techniques and Tactics

Without a doubt, the most useful feed is (as for most species) hemp. Hemp can also be used as a hookbait – either directly on the hook or attached to hair rigs – although I rarely use it as such myself. The main reason for this is that I find it too awkward to make it stay on the hook, and as for hair rigging the stuff, what a nightmare! Assuming that the barbel have got their heads down on the hemp and are ignoring any other offerings, the choice facing you is either to fiddle around with silly things like superglue, or to thread bits of hemp on to cotton and then tie this to the hook. The easiest method in this case, in fact, is to cheat! In every would-be barbel angler's bag there will be a packet or two of little black plastic beads. Simple isn't it? Why not tie these beads on to the hook or, in the case of reverse hair, simply thread them on to the line and fix them above the hook! If you prefer, they can even be glued on to the shank so that they are ready for use. This is far easier than messing around with hemp and is equally as effective.

The main hookbaits I use for barbel are meat – both straight from the tin and in paste form – sweetcorn and maggots. By far the most effective meat has got to be Bacon Grill, with chopped ham and pork run- ning a close second. I find that luncheon meat is the least effective of the meat baits. I use my three favourites along with various seed baits, the most effective of which appear to be tares, maples and peanuts. When using seed baits, it is most important to use high-grade stuff. Ready-prepared seed baits take a lot of beating, as you can be sure that they are both high-grade and cooked correctly. If you choose to prepare your own baits, health food shops are the places to head for. They stock a vast array of suitable seeds for human consumption, and you can be sure that these will not harm the fish – provided they are prepared correctly.

I have caught barbel on many types of baits including, would you believe it, wood-lice. Stick a hook in a wood-lice and see what it looks like – a good imitation of a large hemp seed with legs, don't you think? A much overlooked winter bait is the lobworm, especially during coloured water conditions when the river is starting to fine down from heavy flooding. This, of course, was the method used back in the early days, when prebaiting with thousands of lobs for a number of days before fishing would occasionally produce very large amounts of fish. For the record, the best barbel I have taken on worm is 12lb 12oz, so it is well worth a try. However, I am not suggesting that you invest in thousands of lobs but instead pick the days and conditions to suit.

Some of the biggest barbel recorded have been taken by salmon anglers out of season, having either been hooked in the mouth or foul-hooked somewhere near it. I have had the experience of a large (over 12lb) barbel following a small mepps during the closed season when I was fishing for salmon. I fished for that particular specimen early in the new season using conventional methods, and caught lots of chub but no barbel. Since then, I have tried spinning on the odd occasion but have never taken barbel using this method, although I have taken a few fish early in the season on minnow. Unfortunately, these were not the leviathans I was hoping for. Incidentally, the first recorded capture of Henry (of which more later) was on a minnow, which also took a fish of a mere 14oz later in the same day. It makes you think, doesn't it? I wonder if a campaign using dead or live minnows during the early part of the season would see some good fish on the bank? It probably would, but I doubt that the effort would result in many fish. Generally speaking, I would expect that prebaiting with hemp and your choice of hookbait would produce better results. My own experiments using one rod on minnow and the other rod on recognized baits introduced into the swim, has seen the minnow rod inactive for days at a time whilst fish have come consistently to the other rod. However, I have also observed barbel, including some quite large fish, surging into shoals of minnows and small fry in the closed season.

To conclude, it is worth trying anything as a new bait on your second rod in winter when times are hard, especially one that has a strong smell. Contrary to this generalization, one bait that does seem to produce its fair share of big winter barbel is bread. Personally, I have never caught one using bread, but I have had the odd brief encounter whilst roach fishing. Having said that, an awful lot of large barbel do get landed by people when they are fishing for roach using breadflake in coloured water during warm weather in the winter. Perhaps I ought to step up my tackle when using ledgered bread!

On to rigs. By far the simplest of rigs, and the one I always use when sight fishing for barbel in the summer months, is the running lead. The only thing I tend to do differently from the basic rig is to use a John Roberts boom instead of a swivel. This is only because it makes the changing of weight to suit conditions far easier than having to break the tackle down. By using a suitable sized swivel it can be turned into a bolt rig by forcing the plastic tubing over it. I always tie swivels on to the line and then tie a hook length to them, regardless of whatever hook length material I am using. The alternative ledger stop has no place in any angler's tacklebox. The damage that these cause may well lose you the best fish you have ever hooked. It could be argued that the use of a swivel means that three knots are used, thereby making three weak points in the line. If you are confident enough to tie one knot though, why shouldn't you tie three?

Hair rigs are useful when using seed baits, when cheating as described earlier, or for meat baits in the winter. I do tend to use the hair in conjunction with a bolt rig when using two rods, both in summer when fishing at night or during the winter months when I cannot stalk fish anyway.

A 10lb 6oz fish caught in darkness from the Stour.

For feeder fishing, I use a fixed paternoster rig employing a Drennan ring. The dropper to the feeder has to be relatively short, of course, as otherwise the maggots will tend to wave around too far from the bottom. I find that this rig is more or less tangle-free, no matter how far you want to cast it. The only disadvantage when using rings or swivels for rigs is that should you wish to alter the length of tail, it means tying a new hook length. At times I have used maggots on the hair by tying on a length of fine line armed with a small hook, with its point bent right in to hold the maggots – very useful when you are plagued with eels as you will not tend to hook too many of them. In fact, the only other fish apart from the occasional eel that I have hooked on the hair has been one dace. As for line strength, I rarely use less than 6lb mainline, going up to 8lb for exceptionally weedy or snaggy swims. During the winter months I have even dropped down to 4lb mainline when bites are hard to come by, but I do not like doing this. My hook lengths are nearly always Kryston, although I sometimes use monofilament when maggot fishing in conjunction with small hooks.

I must confess that most of my barbel fishing is done during the summer months these days as other species tend to get in the way during the winter months. This is something that I must try to rectify in future years as I know I am missing out on some excellent chances of large fish – as will be illustrated later. Most barbel anglers and books on the subject will tell you that at first and last light and during the hours of darkness are the best times to catch big fish. I will contradict this here, however, and say that a high percentage of fish I catch seem to come out at the height of the day, including times when it is very bright and not a cloud to be seen. This is probably due to the fact that most of my barbel angling consists of fishing for specimens I have seen, and therefore takes place when visibility is at its best. I must also add that this result also applies to waters that are relatively under-fished – it is often the case that when fishing on popular, heavily fished waters very different results are obtained.

As a consequence of my method, it has now got to the stage that if I cannot find a double during the course of the day then I usually do not fish at all. The task is becoming harder as each season passes as I am not particularly interested in fish that I have already caught unless they are likely to come out at a heavier weight. It is inevitable that on occasions I do have recaptures of barbel whilst in pursuit of other fish. You cannot avoid the possibilities of this happening if there are other fish you wish to catch which inhabit the same length of river, but these recaptures should not be included in your record of the numbers of doubles you have caught.

To some, the way I refer to doubles may indicate that any other fish is just not worth while. This is not the case. While there is a large head of big fish in the area in which I live, I am well aware that other areas are not so well populated with fish.of this size. To put it in perspective, my personal best fish from the Kennet is a fish of 8lb 14oz. To me this is proportionally as good as getting a double from the Avon or Stour. I know that doubles do get caught from the Kennet, and big doubles at that, but there are far fewer fish of equivalent size. In fact, I did spend a considerable amount of time on the Kennet going after a double, but failed. The only rivers that I have taken doubles from are the Avon and Stour, although I did come very close once on the River Colne.

The first fish that I caught on the River Dane in Cheshire was a fish of around 3lb. I was a guest of Steve Jones at the time, and was pleased to catch a barbel at all on the day. Any barbel is a worthwhile quarry when you are fishing away from your home river. There are other rivers in the country than those I have mentioned that do provide anglers with a good head of large fish, and I feel sure that the anglers in these areas also try to single out the larger specimens and, if possible, avoid the capture of smaller fish – assuming that they are able to see their quarry. After all, the quest in my case is to catch large fish and if small fish are to be avoided to this end, then so be it.

Whilst talking about the weight of barbel, it is worth while talking about the fluctuations in barbel weight. In the early part of the season they are likely to be lightest, while at the end of season the fish will be at their best, should they have had the benefit of a reasonably mild winter. To illustrate this phenomenon, I have gathered as much information as possible on some well-known barbel of the Dorset Stour and Hampshire Avon.

Fork in the Tail

As far as I have been able to establish, the first time this fish was caught was by Tim Norman way back in October 1980. At this time the fish weighed 12lb, and he caught the fish twice more in subsequent seasons at 12lb 4oz and 12lb 1oz.

The following year, Terry Lampard caught the fish at 11lb 14oz, and in 1984 Terry caught the fish for a second time at a weight of 11lb 15oz.

In 1985, Kevin Hodges caught the fish at over 12lb before spawning, followed by Greg Buxton who added his name to the list of captors with a weight of 11lb 9oz shortly after the fish had spawned – its lowest weight on record. All the captures at this point were made in the summer and early autumn months. In the same year, Greg caught the fish for a second time in winter conditions in December, and it came to the bank at its best weight to date of 12lb 14oz.

There was then a break as far as is known until 1987 when I added my name to the list for the first time with 12lb 10oz. Some weeks later, Pete Reading added his with 12lb 9oz. I then caught it again during the same season, this time at 12lb 13oz. Once again, these were all summer weights.

The next time of capture, although I know of two anglers who lost the fish in 1989, was in 1990. It was Len Arbery's turn to add his name to the list, and this time Fork in the Tail was at its heaviest. Len managed to get the fish on to the bank at the end of the season, and it weighed in at an impressive 14lb exactly. The fish was in the peak of condition with no loose flesh – as is often evident in the summer months.

The first known capture of Fork in the Tail by Tim Norman in October 1980 when the fish weighed 12lb.

Very early on in the next season Martin Wood added his name to the list with 12lb 8oz, shortly followed by Jamie Stanley at 12lb 4oz. Sadly, this was to be the last known capture of the fish, although there is the distinct possibility that another capture took place shortly after this.

On a bright summer's day whilst fishing on another stretch, John Medlow came down to break the sad news to me. 'I've got Fork in the Tail in the back of my van,' he exclaimed. It transpired that Terry Lampard had spotted what he originally thought was a pike upside-down in a weed-bed. After getting the fish out it turned out to be Fork in the Tail. Assuming that a barbel takes approximately ten to twelve years to make it into double figures, and say perhaps another six or so years to get to 12lb, this fish was likely to have been at least twenty-five years old.

The body of Fork in the Tail is now in a taxidermist's freezer await-
ing its last resting place – encased in a box to be hung from my wall.
This is a sad end to a magnificent barbel, and one that brought so much
joy to its captors!

(Apologies to anyone who caught Fork in the Tail and who has not
appeared on this list.)

The Sopley Fish

My first encounter with the Sopley barbel was in August 1984. There
were a number of barbel in the mill-stream I was fishing, including up
to four doubles. The first one I caught was the mug fish, an obliging
fish that had been caught many times before, although I did not realize this at the time. It was featured in a monthly magazine article enti-
tled 'Kinky but Nice'. In my opinion, I had spotted a fish that looked
about 8–9lb, and as it was the only sizeable fish that I had seen on this
occasion I decided to have a go for it.

The fish was taking bits of meat with total abandon and soon picked
up my offering. I struck rather too hard and smashed the line at the

The Sopley fish at 13lb 2oz.

knot. Within ten minutes it was back in feeding, and on the second pick-up I made no mistake. Once I had it on the bank, I realized that this was no small fish – it registered 11lb 5oz.

I caught this fish again some two weeks later at 10lb 13oz, and it was also caught at least twice by other anglers in the course of a month. It was an old fish well past its prime and at some time would have weighed considerably more. The reason for my initial underestimation as to the size of this fish was that it was shaped somewhat like a bow, losing a lot of its length when in the water. It was kinked so much (hence the name of the magazine article) that the lower edge of its tail was considerably worn away.

Three days after my initial encounter with this fish, I spotted another fish in the same swim. I had been baiting three areas and had a fish of around 10lb feeding, although not confidently, in a swim upstream. I had come down to check the other two swims and found the mug fish and another feeding on the meat. In fact, soon none of the meat I had thrown in was left. I quickly got my tackle from the other swim and tossed in a few more offerings – these were taken almost as soon as they hit the bottom. I dropped in a piece of meat on a size 4 hook and the new fish picked it up. I made no mistakes, and it was safely on the bank to weigh in at 11lb 8oz. I had one other fish from this stretch worth mentioning – the one from the upstream swim which turned out to be a low ten-pounder. Having found nothing else worth bothering with, I left the stretch.

In 1987 and towards the end of the season, I noticed a picture of Dave Charles holding a 12lb 12½oz barbel in the *Angling Times*. I recognized this as the 11lb 8oz fish from Sopley, and decided to have another go for it. In the afternoon of 3 March, and after being there since mid-morning, I caught it for the second and last time at 13lb 2oz. At the time this was my personal best barbel, and it was in the peak of winter condition. The capture was from exactly the same position in the same swim, once again on meat, the only difference being that I had used a hair and bolt rig on this occasion. For the record, my witness Mike Lamb caught it again in August during the next season at 11lb exactly – a winter–summer fluctuation of 2lb 2oz.

Henry

Henry must be one of the better known barbel in Britain. As far as I have been able to establish, the first known capture of Henry was by Martin Elliott in 1972. This was on a free-lined minnow and the fish then weighed 9lb 2oz. No known captures were recorded until 1980 when it was taken for its first time in double figures, as far as is known, by Kevin Hodges at a weight of 12lb 6oz. This gap of eight years had added 3lb to its weight. The list of anglers who have caught Henry since includes: Terry Lampard a number of times with a best weight of 13lb 11oz; Greg Buxton who caught the fish at its then best ever weight of 14lb 1oz in October 1985 (it had therefore taken another five years to gain less than 2lb); Pete Reading and myself who both caught Henry at 14lb 2oz in 1987 (I also had the fish twice during the following season at 13lb 11oz and 13lb 3oz); Pete Young who had it in 1990 at 12lb 2oz; and finally both Richard Graham and Andy Harman who caught it at a weight of 13lb exactly in the same season. Again, there are possibly others that I have missed. The latest in the season that Henry has been caught as far as I know, however, was when Greg had it at 14lb 1oz in October 1985.

My first encounter with Henry was a result of the fact that I had decided that it was about time that I caught it myself. I started off on the river from 16 March, knowing roughly the area from which it had been caught, and started off at midnight in a deep pool in which I had

Henry, one of the better known barbel in Britain, at 14lb 2oz.

seen a good fish during the closed season (this was not Henry). This pool saw me off to a good start and got me used to what was going to be the norm for this stretch – I blanked!

Not to be beaten, I continued in my quest for Henry and some two weeks into the season I spotted a very large barbel on some shallows below the deep swim. Again, this was not Henry but another fish of larger proportions and one that I estimated at over 15lb. I did manage to hook this fish, only to lose it when it got itself into a piece of barbed wire on the bottom of a very fast run. I was to have a further encounter with this fish some two seasons later, with a similar end result, but I digress. A week or so after the loss of the large fish, I finally spotted Henry in one of the swims that I had been baiting with hemp and corn.

It was almost casual in its approach to the swim, moving across it some 3ft off the bottom. I had not seen this behaviour in a barbel before but paid no particular attention to it, such was my impatience to get a bait in the water. This was the first of many mistakes. It became apparent to me why the fish was behaving in this manner, but it was too late when I noticed the fish coming across the weed, only to hit the line with its outstretched pectoral fin. It moved back out of the swim in a very leisurely manner, swam off upstream and was not spotted again for over a week.

We spent the following months playing a game of cat and mouse. Seven times I thought I had got it right, only to miss on the strike. Each time I missed Henry, whether the fish had hit the line or spooked it in some other way, I would fish for other barbel or a different species for a few days. I would then return for another attempt, but the game always seemed to end in Henry's favour.

In September 1987 I finally got it right. I arrived late in the afternoon to find the swim positively glowing. Three days earlier I had piled 2 gallons of hemp and around 4 pints of hookbaits straight into the middle of the main weed-bed. The reasons for this were purely selfish – I had to work in Cornwall for a few days and had no chance of getting back until I had finished the job. The evening before I left, Henry came into the swim as it was turning dark and started to feed like there was no tomorrow. I knew that if anyone came down the following day it was more than likely that Henry would come out. The chances of catching Henry after dark, however, were remote, so I had to take drastic action. With this in mind, I piled the bait directly into a weed-bed, hoping to feed Henry up for a few days, by keeping the bait under the weed-bed and out of sight.

On my arrival back in Dorset I went straight to the river. Henry was under the weed and just out of sight. I threw in a couple of handfuls of hemp and a few hookbaits. Within minutes, Henry was out munching happily on the freebies. Having seen my car, Dave Tissington arrived and headed over for a chat. I pointed Henry out and we both watched for a while whilst I waited for Henry to go out of the swim. The reason I waited for the fish to leave was, as previous experiences had shown, that if I were to cast in while Henry was in the swim, that would be enough to spook it. After about five minutes Henry left the clear gravel area of the swim munching a mouthful of food, and went back under the weed. This was my chance.

Quickly, I cast in my offering on a two swan shot link ledger in a position I thought would be in the path of Henry as it came back out from beneath the weed. Indeed, Henry came out from the weed soon after I had cast in and moved across to the bait. I watched as it mouthed and finally picked up the bait, then I banged the hook home. The rod heaved over, but I gave the fish no line whatsoever as it proceeded to demolish the smaller weed-bed in front of me. Dave offered to land the fish but I declined, pointing out that if it was to be lost at the net I would rather it was my mistake. The fight was impressive to say the least, and it was with great relief that the fish eventually went into the waiting net. Once on the bank, the hookhold proved to be very light – in fact, only around ¼in – with the point of the hook protruding from the fleshy part of the bottom lip. Had I have known the hookhold was so poor I would not have been quite so aggressive! It is unusual to hook a barbel in this manner, and most of the time the hook point will not show. The reason for the light hooking this time may have been because the fish was about to eject the bait as I struck.

The scales were zeroed with the wet weigh sling, and Henry pulled them down to register slightly over 14lb 2oz. This had beaten my previous best, the Sopley fish, by slightly over one pound. I do not tend to count fractions of ounces, and so settled for a weight of 14lb 2oz. Richard Graham was called out as a second witness, and after photographs were taken Henry was returned to the water.

Henry has never been taken at the end of the season and I am sure that if it had been, it would have taken the record to at least 15lb and possibly even 16lb going by the general summer/winter statistical fluctuations of other fish. Sadly, Henry now appears to be in decline, having been caught recently at its lowest weight for years at 12lb 2oz by Pete Young. It was not for some months after Pete caught the fish that we realized it was Henry as its condition had changed considerably from when it was in its prime during the mid- to late 1980s. The backbone of the fish now appeared to be bowlike and is showing through the flesh – rather reminiscent of the Sopley mug fish, which has been missing and presumed dead for some years now. The signs are that Henry has not many years left in it and, no doubt it will either be found dead or will disappear in the not-too-distant future. Still, maybe I will be proved wrong and it might recover enough to beat 14lb again – I hope so, but the signs are against it.

The age of Henry would appear to be in excess of thirty years going on the information gathered from its first capture and subsequent growth rates up to 1987. This assumes that it took around ten years to reach 9lb 2oz, plus a growing age of some twenty-three years up to, say, 1985.

Richard Graham's Fourteen

This fish has got to rate as the finest example of a barbel in prime condition ever taken, and due credit must be given to the captor for achieving something that we would all like to do. Never before, as far as we know, had this fish seen the bank. The measurements of the fish, the weight and the photographs were taken by myself, the measurements being as follows: length 29¾in; maximum girth, 18½in; and girth just above the vent, over 17in. To say that this was an impressive fish is an understatement, and Richard himself has recorded the capture of this fish below.

Richard Graham's Account of His Personal Best
During the summer of 1988 I decided it was about time I caught a double-figure barbel. Having lived in Dorset for most of my life I felt that I should really have had one by then. The Dorset Stour and the Hampshire Avon are within easy reach of my home, and these rivers are well known for the amount of doubles that they hold. Both rivers had produced a number of barbel to my rods; but it seemed that my choice of venues and use of the non-selective fishing methods were possible reasons why the size of these fish remained average. The best fish I had landed by then was 9lb.

Fishing in areas with a high population of barbel had proved immense fun, but the chances of my catching a leviathan remained relatively slim. A change of method and venue seemed to be the answer. The lower density stretches would offer a far better chance of catching the calibre of fish I was after, and speculation on this method of location brought two particular stretches to mind. One of these already had a good track record, with fish of 12lb having been caught in previous seasons; to my knowledge, the other had no such history. I spent a considerable amount of time from the middle of the closed season onward fish spotting. Although the amount of barbel I saw in the unknown stretch during this time was low, the average size of the barbel appeared to be high, and this, coupled with the fact that this section was not heavily fished, made it the best choice for my new approach.

When the season started, fishing through the summer months proved to be extremely exhilarating but also very frustrating! This was mainly due to the large number of ravenous chub that seemed to devour my offerings of hemp and corn – they proved impossible to feed off no matter how much bait I threw at them. To compensate for this, the few barbel that I did manage to tempt proved to be worthwhile, including three doubles topped by a fish of 11lb 6oz. This fish was caught whilst stalking at a time when the swim in question held six barbel. In my estimation, four of these fish appeared to be over the magic 10lb mark and one looked considerably larger than the fish I had caught so far. From then on, this swim demanded far more attention than the other swims I had been fishing, eventually excluding the rest altogether.

On 3 October, I found myself fishing this swim once again. The weather was not conducive to stalking and I was forced to fish blind. From previous experiences I knew this method was not particularly selective as the chub would be the most likely fish to show first in the swim. When this does occur, the barbel are most unlikely to feed with any confidence and the chances of success are vastly reduced.

I baited the swim with loose-fed hemp and a handful of maple peas. I cast in and awaited the first bite – which I expected to come from the resident chub within minutes. Surprisingly, after forty minutes or so nothing had happened, and then I had a 6in pull on the tip which took me by surprise – I missed it! On retrieving the tackle (which I had somehow managed to embed in the bottom of the river) I found that I had damaged the hook. As the light was fading fast and it had started to rain heavily I was tempted to call it a day, but instead decided to tie a new hook and give it one final cast.

I cast back into the swim and made myself as comfortable as I could in the adverse conditions. Minutes later the rod was pulled round again, and this time my reflexes were quicker. The strike met with solid resistance and I felt a powerful fish move steadily downstream. This was most definitely a barbel! The fish moved out into the flow and turned back up toward me as it succumbed to the pressure I was exerting.

The fight was slow and dogged, as had proved most usual in my limited experience of large barbel, but I kept the pressure on and the barbel steadily came nearer. After approximately five minutes, the barbel appeared over the rim of the waiting landing net which I lifted to bring the fish safely to the bank. Once there, I realized that this was an exceptionally large fish. I tried to weigh it but could not obtain an accurate reading as my hands were shaking too much! As I knew where Martin was fishing that night I decided to sack the fish, staying with it for some time to ensure that everything would be all right, and then go and get him.

Both he and Dave Tissington, who was also on this water, duly made the trek back to where the fish was sacked. Both had asked the weight of the barbel but I was only able to confirm that it was easily in excess of 13lb. When we arrived back at the swim Martin

Success for Richard Graham – and what a fish!

got all the camera gear and scales ready before removing the fish from the sack, saying as he did so that was very close to 14lb. This proved to be a very accurate estimation, for on lifting the fish into the weigh sling, the scales registered slightly over 14lb. We settled on a final weight of 14lb exactly, and the fish was duly photographed.

I took the fish back to the water to return it to its habitat. Concern for its welfare had become the main priority at this point as although it was not showing any serious signs, it appeared to be in some distress. It refused to keep itself upright and was blowing air from its mouth and gills, but after a considerable amount of time – during which both myself and Martin took turns in the water with the fish – it started to recover.

We kept the fish supported in the water for a good half-hour before finally releasing it. We were still concerned for it, and Martin shone a torch on it for a further hour before it made its way under a weed bed. Safe in the knowledge that the barbel was now perfectly fit, we retired to the nearest public house to celebrate with a few well-earned beers.

I myself caught this fish in August 1990 at a summer weight of 11lb 15oz. It was my third barbel from this particular stretch – I had caught a 10lb 13oz barbel the previous day, and my best from the water at 12lb 7oz nearly two years earlier in late October 1988. Incidentally, this fish had not been caught before and it has not been on the bank since I caught it as far as we know. Again we have a weight fluctuation of over 2lb for Richard's fish.

Most of the fish in this stretch of the river seem to show very similar shaped pectoral fins. A question that comes to mind is do they have the same parents, as this seems to be unique to this stretch and the density of barbel is very low? Only in recent years has there been any marked increase in fish of less than around 8lb in weight. These also tend to have similar shaped fins, suggesting that they are the offspring of their larger brethren. Perhaps another case of a few fish stocked at one time?

From this information it would be relatively safe to assume that any barbel in a typical summer 'spawned out' condition that made it to, say, over 12lb is capable of breaking the record – that is, if it is a healthy fish. (I am inclined to say that it should be a young fish, but find it hard to determine definitely at what stage a fish becomes old and in decline.)

A fabulous 12lb 7oz fish – the first in eight years on this particular stretch.

No doubt there are fish from these and other rivers that could easily be added to this list, but I have merely used these particular fish to illustrate a point. In turn, this gives rise to speculation as to how many fish over 14lb are swimming around in our rivers at the back end of the season.

On heavily fished stretches of a river it is generally assumed that all the fish are known, having been caught before. I totally disagree with this. Having seen the behaviour of larger-than-average fish in visible waters I feel that any fish, and barbel in particular, can avoid capture for most, if not all of their lives. I have seen some exceptionally large fish in both the Stour and Avon that have never been caught. In the winter of 1991 on a well-fished water which falls into the category of 'every fish has been caught before', Mike Lamb had a fish of over 12lb which had not been on the bank before. It may well have moved into the stretch from elsewhere shortly before this capture, but bear in mind that various clubs and syndicates control the fishing for at least six miles above and below this stretch. As far as is known, this fish has not been taken from any of these venues.

On certain stretches of the Hampshire Avon in particular, fishing during the hours of darkness is very limited. This is probably a contributing factor in why large fish are able to avoid capture – it will not take them long to become conditioned to the fact that as darkness falls the anglers have to leave. I am sure plenty of anglers have fished all day, only to see barbel moving in to mop up the bait they have been throwing in just as they are forced to pack up. I am sure that there are stretches on the Avon that would certainly throw up a few surprises should an angler be able to gain even a couple of hours' fishing after dark.

Where to Fish

Barbel distribution on the Avon is widespread, from the lower river right through to beyond Salisbury. One of the most well-publicized fisheries is, of course, the Royalty at Christchurch. Whilst the Royalty does hold a fair stock of barbel, the average size is low. There are,

Henry at 13lb.

59

however, still a few doubles to be caught. The very nature of its past reputation means that during the summer months you are unlikely to have much chance in a choice of swims and will end up fishing amongst a lot of people. After October, the numbers start to fall dramatically, giving you far more freedom to move about and spot a few fish – should conditions allow.

No doubt, you will at some stage have a look into the Parlour Pool. The barbel in here are very obliging at showing themselves at the top of the pool above the chain. Particularly during the latter part of the closed season, these barbel will take anything you care to throw at them from right under your nose. People will lead you to believe that there are monsters well over the record to be had here, and you will probably even be able to see these 'record' fish at very close quarters. The trouble is that a fish that most people estimate at anything from 14lb upward will in fact only weigh 11–12lb depending on the time of year it is caught. Similarly, its fellow companions will be of considerably less weight. Sometime in the not too distant past, however, there was a very large barbel in Parlour Pool which was well over the record. It was never caught, and sadly it is now missing and presumed dead.

Most of the doubles that are in the Royalty are well-known fish, having been caught many times before. My best barbel and only double from here was a 12lb 12oz fish which I landed way back in 1983. Again, this was a known fish which is also on the missing list now. I do still fish the Royalty on occasion these days, but for species other than barbel.

Despite all this, the Royalty is a good bet for a reasonable day's fishing at any time of the year. Barbel even show during conditions well below freezing, although the Royalty is somewhat unique in this respect and I would not recommend trying to catch barbel elsewhere during these periods. The fishery is steeped in nostalgia, with named pools (such as the Railway where the present record came from) having been mentioned in the writing of many, and is a nice place for a visiting angler to spend a day's fishing.

The most prolific stretches of the Avon are in the middle section around the Ringwood area, mostly controlled by the Ringwood and Christchurch angling clubs. Both clubs offer day ticket facilities for visiting anglers which can be obtained from Ringwood Tackle on the banks of the Avon. The fishing in this area offers both the pleasure angler and the big-fish man excellent sport. The Avon at this point is a highly visible water, lending itself perfectly to stalking individual fish or to finding a group to spend the day after.

Above Ringwood day tickets become sparse, with most of the water being under club control or syndicated. The barbel populations themselves also become thinner, and the higher up the Avon that you go the less fish, in general, you are likely to find. Possibly the last place that you are in with a reasonable chance of catching barbel is at Britford just below Salisbury. This stretch is controlled and owned by the London Anglers' Association. Barbel were introduced here during the 1960s or 1970s, although I am not sure exactly when. They have survived and spawned with limited success. The best fish to have come from this stretch weighed over 13lb, with a fair number of back-up fish also taken. My best from this water was a 10lb 3oz fish taken in 1990, and in fact this was the only fish that I have caught here, although I have spotted a number of other fish on the venue.

There have been fish reported above this water but these are few and far between. The highest point at which I have heard of fish being taken was actually from a tributary of the Avon, the River Nadder in the Churchfields area just above the city. The reports were of two fish to the same angler in one day, both sevens. I know the angler concerned and have no reason to doubt the authenticity of the report.

The River Stour population is not as far extended as the Avon but offers excellent fishing in its lower reaches. The most famous of these is the Throop Fishery's section in Bournemouth, again a popular day ticket fishery which is very busy during the summer months. The Stour is of a totally different character to its faster flowing sister river, being a mainly clay-based river rather than having the chalk-based bed of the Avon. The Stour tends to clear later in the season than the Avon due to both suspended solids and its tendency to suffer periodically from algal blooms throughout the summer months. Nevertheless, spotting is easier than on the Avon owing to the fact that the banks are generally higher than those of the Avon and the flow is less. Also, there tends to be far more trees along its banks which afford good vantage points for the agile angler.

Dealing with Throop Fishery first, there are a number of sizeable fish throughout the length of the water. Named swims such as the Ladder Tree, Gallery and Barbel Corner, to mention but a few, offer both confidence and inspire the visiting angler in his or her quest. The possibility of a double is high anywhere along its entire length. Thirteen-pound fish have been caught in recent years with a good number of back-up fish to keep the big-fish man happy. The numbers of smaller fish – averaging 7lb – is also high, so the possibility of taking a large amount of fish from this water in a day is good.

With hemp banned at both Throop and the Royalty, either meat, corn or maggot are the best choices of bait. The fish do see an awful lot of meat but tend to become wary of it as the season progresses. Whilst hemp is banned, there is nothing in the rules to say that you cannot use other seed baits on the stretch and certainly maples fished over tares can be well worth a try when meat fishing becomes hard. The reasoning behind the banning of hemp on these waters is somewhat outdated, and I feel that it may be allowed again on Throop in the not-too-distant future.

In the lower reaches of Throop the river becomes tidal. Whilst there are barbel well down below Throop, very few are ever caught – mainly due to the fact that no one actually fishes for them. I have spent the odd day below Iford with some success in the shape of fish to around 9lb, but aesthetically speaking the river at this point becomes rather hostile.

Above Throop the river is controlled again by Ringwood and Christchurch angling clubs, along with Wimborne, and includes the

Rob Shallcroft with his first Avon barbel at 9lb 12 oz.

odd free stretch. Day ticket stretches, apart from Throop, do not exist on the Stour until you get well above the main barbel population. There are a number of doubles and some very good fishing to be had in the waters of both Christchurch and Ringwood angling clubs, along with the free stretch at Musscliffe and opposite the Bridge House Hotel below Longham Waterworks.

Once past the waterworks, barbel populations become very thin. Pockets of fish do exist right up to Blandford and were introduced in the early 1980s as far up as Fiddleford. Only one fish has been taken from above Blandford, as far as is known at a weight of 7lb in 1988 – this was probably one of the fish from Fiddleford Mill that had moved downstream. There have been fish sighted in Blandford Weir on odd occasions, and I myself lost a good fish from Rookery Island below Spetisbury whilst dace fishing in the winter of 1983.

The Stour changes character above Longham. While below the weir most of the river bed is visible, or any deep holes are not particularly long in length, once above the weir there are vast expanses of water that you cannot see into owing to long tracts of water over 7ft deep. In these sections barbel could go undetected for years. It would take a very brave soul to fish in one of these sections for a season without knowing if barbel were present. Even in sections that fit this category, but which have barbel in evidence above and below, it would be a daunting task. I for one have not the courage to attempt what could easily be a fruitless mission.

I have fished for barbel in a number of rivers other than the Stour and Hampshire Avon, including the Severn, Dane, Kennet, Loddon, Colne, Bristol Avon, Medway, Wey and Thames. Apart from the Medway and Thames, I caught fish from all of them. There are others that I would like to get round to if I can find time, but with the Avon and Stour holding so many good fish it becomes difficult to move on to other waters when I feel that I have access to some of the very best fishing in the country on my own doorstep. One river that I feel I must get round to fishing, however, is the Wye. The Wye seems like a larger version of the Hampshire Avon in its appearance and would appear to be a good stalking river.

Where is the next record barbel going to come from? I feel that any rich river in Britain is capable of producing a record fish, with favoured rivers being (not in any particular order): the Hampshire and Bristol Avons; the Stour; the Wye; the Severn or its tributaries; the Great Ouse; and the Medway. The former record of 14lb 6oz has been equalled by fish from the Hampshire Avon and the Medway recently, and the Medway fish has gone on to record weights of 14lb 9oz and 14lb 13oz.

One last comment. When any barbel – particularly a large fish taken in summer – is returned to the water, be extremely vigilant when the fish finally moves away from your hands. It is far better to spend a lot of time with the fish and, if possible, to monitor it for a while after it has swum away than to assume that it will be all right. The fact that a large fish is likely to be a number of years older than a superfit eight-pounder means that it may well turn up in the weed and choke on silt. On occasion, I have had to go in after fish up to fifteen minutes or so after capture and release, especially in the case of larger fish when hot summer conditions have dictated that oxygen levels were low. To make a point, Fork in the Tail was often a difficult fish to put back. Its captors, myself included, have had problems with this fish in the past, and there is a possibility that the fish was caught by an inexperienced angler prior to its death. So please take every precaution possible, and follow the guide-lines below on how to deal with barbel.

1. Immediately after capture, weigh and then sack the fish, ensuring that it is facing the right way, then stay with it until you are absolutely sure it is able to keep itself upright.
2. Get all photographic gear ready to hand, ensuring that you have enough film for the job in the camera. Decide where the pictures will be taken before removing the fish from the water. Be aware that the fish may well have recovered sufficiently to be a bit of a handful, and with this in mind remove the fish from the sack whilst kneeling down. Be prepared for any sudden movements, and if control of the fish is in any doubt make sure you get it down on to the sack rather than dropping it. Take your photos quickly.
3. Take the fish back to the water in the sack or weigh sling if any distance is to be covered. Hold the fish facing upstream, preferably in flowing water. Do not allow the fish to swim away until you are absolutely sure it is able to do so. If at all possible, keep an eye on it to make sure it does not turn over.

I make no apologies for these guide-lines, and although I have used the barbel as a prime example, they should be applied in part to all fish. I know that most anglers will find these points obvious, but those who have never caught a barbel may not necessarily understand their idiosyncrasies. On occasion, I have had to help some anglers with the return of their barbel as they lacked experience with the species, and I feel that if the guide-lines above save the life of just one barbel or a fish of any other species, I am completely justified in including them!

4

Chub

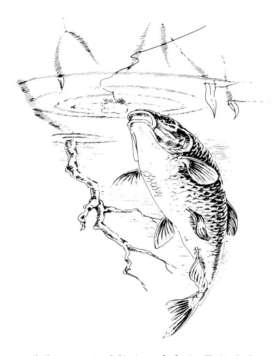

Chub must be one of the most obliging fish in Britain's waters. They seem to feed in the most varied of conditions – including sub-zero temperatures – but although they can be caught in great numbers during the course of a day's fishing, they are often easily spooked. Once they are aware of the fact that you are there, it may be extremely difficult to get the larger fish to feed. Accordingly, the approach to chub fishing has to be undertaken with extreme caution. Even in heavy water conditions a clumsy approach down the banks of the river will alert the chub to your presence, and although they may not move too far away from their chosen swim their willingness to feed is sure to be greatly reduced. Often the larger and more wary fish will not be tempted at all in these circumstances.

Anyway, enough of the doom and gloom when in search of chub, let us assume that we are in with a chance. If your idea of chub fishing is to attempt to empty a swim in the hope that you will land a large fish, then I am afraid that your success rate is going to be extremely low. It is far better to locate an individual fish, or groups of fish that are of a larger-than-average weight. I consider a good chub to be anything over 5lb in weight. I know that many anglers reading this will disagree and think that 4lb is a good fish, and I must say that I completely agree if you are fishing anywhere other than my local Dorset Stour or Hampshire Avon. Note that I am about talking river chub now – there are pits in this area and, indeed, all over the country with large chub present, and I have taken fish up to 5lb 9oz from a stillwater near Bournemouth.

A 4lb 5oz Avon chub caught in the winter.

Most of my chub fishing is done on rivers, so I will deal with these first. My main regret here is that during my obsession with barbel I landed several large chub that I never bothered to weigh. And now the prologue. It came to pass, one day whilst I was unhooking a chub someone suggested that I weighed it. Under protest I did, and that fish weighed 4lb 14oz. I wonder what some of the ones I had put back previously might have weighed? I then decided to adopt a policy of weighing chub that looked as if they might weigh over 5lb. The funny thing is that it took around three years to get one.

The Hampshire Avon once again is becoming an extremely good chub river. At one time it was probably the best chub river in Britain, but during the earlier years that I fished it (early 1980s) the chub were heavily infested with the hookworm parasite *Pomphorhynchus laevis*. This nasty piece of work attaches itself to the intestinal walls of the fish, thereby living off the food that otherwise would be feeding the fish. The result of this infestation is that although the chub will still attain its usual length, it will be underweight for its size. Some of the reason for this heavy infestation may well have lain in the water authority's excessive weed-cutting programme.

As with the majority of parasites, the hookworm parasite uses more than one host during its lifespan, the freshwater shrimp being

The author cradles a 4lb 6oz chub.

another such host. Cutting the weed so dramatically provided the chub with a glut of shrimp and, chub being what they are, they ate as many of these during this period as they could. The end result was that far larger amounts of parasites were ingested than would otherwise have been eaten. (This is by no means restricted to chub, as the barbel during this time also suffered from the same parasite.) In recent years, however, due to the lowering of the water table – thanks to excessive water abstraction combined with lower annual rainfall – the water authority has cut the weed far less than they once did. Gone are the days when you could be forgiven for thinking you may have gone to the wrong river, as once again there is now weed and 4ft or more extra depth of water in which to fish. This means that the chub no longer have the majority of their annual intake of shrimps all in one go. The Avon chub of the 1990s are on their way back up! One only has to look at the angling press to see the amount of five-, six- and (occasionally) seven-pounders that appear periodically throughout the season.

From the previous paragraph one may assume that I am happy to blame the water authority for all the problems of the Hampshire Avon. However, although they certainly are a contributing factor to present-day problems, they cannot be attributed with all the blame. The reasons for the decline of any river are often varied, with many factors to be taken into consideration. Pollution, whether from chemicals dumped or inadvertently spilt, farm or sewage effluent and many other sources, are all there waiting to take their toll on the fish stocks. If you come across any form of pollution you should contact the Anglers' Co-operative Association (*see* Useful Addresses), although it never ceases to amaze me that with angling regarded as the largest participant sport in Britain the Association's membership numbers are still pathetically low – a mere 15,000 at the beginning of 1992. Each and every one of us should be a member as this is the only body that is dedicated to fight for us against the polluters, and I urge you to join! Anyway, enough said and on with the book.

The chub on the Avon were, at the time I started to fish it in 1980, extremely long and thin. I do not think I was alone in regarding them as not worth weighing, and I just returned them to the water. It must have been sometime during the mid-1980s that chub started getting back to their former selves. Around this time I was fishing for barbel with Rob Castle on the middle Avon. It was rather a hot day and I had fallen asleep in my chair whilst waiting for the pin to wake me from my dreams. However, it was not the pin but Rob that woke me up.

Rob Castle catches one of the early Avon 5lb fish at an
ounce over the mark.

'Come and take a photo of this 5lb chub,' he said. I told him to go away in no uncertain terms as there were no fours on the Avon, never mind fives. He was very insistent and I forced myself to go and weigh the fish. Sure enough it was a 5lb fish! I put this down to a fluke and dismissed it, but it may actually have been the turning point for the chub as over the next season or two more and more chub started to reach more healthy weights.

The River Stour, on the other hand, was not affected by the hookworm parasite to any such degree and offered a much better chance of a decent fish. In the early 1980s when I fished the Stour around the Blandford area, I spent a lot of time going after chub during the week when the distances involved in searching out barbel were a bit cost-prohibitive. I found that the most successful bait was crayfish, and I caught a lot of large fours on this bait but never a five. This was mostly due to the fact that I never managed to find one whilst I had a bucket of crays.

The way a chub hits a crayfish has to be experienced to be appreciated. By far the best method to fish with these is to cast at seen fish. It was by chance, however, that I discovered the best place to cast the crayfish to the chub. A bad cast resulted in my free-lined bait dropping into the water some 3ft behind the fish, but the resulting bite, or dare I say take, was so savage that the rod was nearly torn from my hand. From then on I always adopted this method of approach when using crayfish, the advantage being that I could now creep up on a seen fish and cast up to it rather than inching the bait down as I had been doing before. This meant that the chub were less likely to spot me as I had no need to move above them.

Which Bait?

There are two methods of collecting crayfish. The first is rather boring and uses a dropnet – that strange, circular net which is used for collecting crabs, shrimps and the like from piers. Bait the net with a nice smelly fish and drop it into the run-off of a weirpool at night. After a pint or three in the local pub, return an hour or so later and pull the net up quickly. Hey presto! Lot of crayfish. If you have any more than three pints the likelihood of falling in the weir goes up, so the moral is: do not drink and collect crays at the same time!

Now on to the fun method. Get yourself a small landing net (it must be triangular with a short pole), a suitable bucket half-full of water and a heavy stick . . . no, we are not going to beat them to death! Pick a sunny day and go back to the same weirpool and get in the water. Oh yes, you will also need a pair of suitable polarizing glasses, so go back to your car. Right, are we all ready now?

Start by turning over the larger flat stones whilst watching for any movements. Once you spot a cray, show it the stick by putting it in the water a foot or so in front of it. This will keep its attention while you slowly position the net about a foot behind it. Now move the stick sharply toward the cray – it will disappear into the net faster than your eye can register. Pull the net up swiftly in a forward motion and remove the cray, placing it into the waiting bucket. I forgot to mention something else . . . those claws are sharp aren't they? When catching crayfish in this manner you gain an understanding as to why chub hit them so hard – if they took a more leisurely approach then it is more than likely that it would result in a missed meal!

The most important thing that I did not mention here, however, is that the British crayfish is now a protected species. I am not sure if you can use imported American crays or not, but I suppose that if they are in the river system then you can – that is, if you can tell the difference.

I bet if you can't tell the difference the person who catches you using the wrong ones can!

If you do not intend using crays for fear of prosecution, then good natural alternatives include slugs (the big black ones), worms (preferably lobs), and any other grubs or insects found on the banks or on trees overhanging the river. With slugs the only time when they will really work is when they are actually seen on the bank. You may be successful when they are not around on occasion, but generally this is very much a 'sometime' bait in these circumstances.

Recently, I have been told of a way to make the slugs more succulent. As most of our gardens contain a fair amount of slugs and a compost heap, it stands to reason that most of the slugs will be in or around this compost and living on the decaying vegetable matter. Apparently, however, slugs have a taste for watermelon and the method is to cut one of these in half and place the two halves facing down on top of the heap in the evening. By the morning the resident slugs will have gorged themselves and will still be under the melon halves. The slugs obtained using this method are the fattest I have ever seen, and fished in the same manner as crays they can be a very effective bait.

Worms work best when the water is coloured, the method to use being touch ledgering in all the likely spots and adopting a mobile approach. If you decide to be a bit lazy, a rod rest and quivertip can be employed. Also, if you decide to use two rods then the quivertip is most useful as the softer action of the tip will give a far better indication of a bite, while offering less resistance to a wary fish. You will therefore have a better chance of hooking it.

Now, on to grubs, caterpillars and the like. A now much-neglected art is dapping, which is the most successful method when using these baits. It calls for the most stealthy approach of the lot. At certain times of the year various insects will be climbing around on the branches of trees overhanging the river. Inevitably, some of these insects end up falling into the river, and when they do so the chub become preoccupied in taking them. All you have to do is collect a few after observing a good chub feeding in this manner, and then present it to the fish.

This method of presentation calls for a long rod, a single suitably sized hook and an ability to crawl on your belly. Basically, after hooking the said grub, allow a short length of line (around a couple of feet) to dangle from the end of the rod. Then inch your way toward where the chub is feeding and slowly lower the bait to the waiting fish. It is quite amazing how a chub reacts to this method, and the slower you lower the bait in, the more frenzied the chub becomes – so much so that it sometimes boils on the surface. As the bait is about to hit the water, lower the rod quickly and the chub will grab it as swiftly as it can. I would advise you to use a pin for this type of fishing as the necessary strike will cause the chub to belt off at an alarming rate. If you use a fixed-spool reel then the chances are that owing to the short length of line you will be broken off before you have had the chance to back-wind.

One of the best times to capitalize on this method is in late September when the wasps are getting stupefied on tree sap. They seem to get extremely drunk in their overindulgent thirst for this stuff and do a lot of falling in (rather like the man who drank too much while catching crayfish by the boring method!) If you can bring yourself to pick up these lovely creatures without being stung in the process, then a lot of chub will come your way. Alternatively, collect a few wasp nests and fish with the grubs which are in the advanced stages – I suppose I should now go on to tell you how to collect wasp nests!

First, you will need a suitable poison which will enable you to kill the adult wasps without harming the grubs, a long stick with a spoon attached to the end so that you can place the poison around the entrance to the nest, and a garden fork. Then, of course, you need to know where a nest is, but how do you find one? Basically, what you need to do is to get your running shoes on, sit in an area you know wasps frequent, and then watch for wasps that are flying in a straight line. If you see wasps carrying anything and drop it whilst in flight, they are moving away from the nest – which should not be far away. The ones flying in a straight line that are carrying anything that they do not drop are the wasps that you have to follow. These are the workers returning with their spoils to feed the grubs and the queen back at the nest. As soon as you spot a carrying wasp, you must follow it until you either lose it or an obstacle gets in your way. All you have to do then is follow the next wasp and so on until you find the entrance to the nest. This operation can be repeated until you have found a few nests and have noted their positions.

When you have chosen your nest, lace the entrance of it with poison about an hour before dark – at this time all the workers will be heading back for a night's sleep. Leave the nest well alone until an hour or so after dark when it can be dug out. If you are lucky, all the adult wasps will be dead at this stage, but often a few are still alive. It is worth pointing out here that although they may be dead they can still sting you, so heavy gardening-type gloves should be worn throughout the operation. If you are a brave soul, or don't know anyone in the

A super-looking 5½lb fish. The question is though, who is the angler?
The author has waited for years to be contacted about this photograph.

pest extermination business from which to get the necessary poison, then you will have no choice but to dig the nest out after dark. A bee-keeper's hat, suit and gloves are a must if you are going to avoid getting stung. Once the nests have been removed they should be placed into a polythene bag and put into your freezer complete. Once the wasp nest has been in the freezer for a while all the wasps in it will be dead, providing you with baits ranging from grubs right through to adults. It is a lot of hard work but well worth it as the rewards can be excellent.

Both the grubs and the cake from the nest can be used as bait. The grubs may be used as described above or in similar ways to maggots, although they tend to be a bit soft and don't stand up to heavy casting. The cake itself can be used as a floater which can be very effective when a few bits are allowed to drift down with the current.

Pre-baiting with seed baits will attract a lot of chub of all sizes. Hemp is the most useful and cheapest of baits, especially if purchased in bulk direct from a seed merchant instead of through you local tackle shop – sorry Ted! (if you cannot cook the stuff at home or if money is no object, then go and see Ted – I am sure he will be happy to

73

accommodate you!). Vast numbers of chub can be concentrated into an area that has seen a quantity of bait going in over a period of time.

Seeds for hookbaits are so numerous that it would take quite a few lines to list them all, so I will only mention one – maple peas! These must be the most successful seed baits when it comes to chub. It does not seen to matter if you fish a water that has never seen a maple in its history as the chub will take them almost the instant that they are introduced. The best condition in which to use them seems to be when they are over a week old, sticky and a little on the high side, as bites are positive and easily hit. At first you can use them directly on the hook but, as usual, the hair rig has to come into play after a time.

Other useful methods of taking chub in the summer months are with minnows and artificial flies, plugs or spinners. In the early weeks of the season minnows are extremely effective. The usual method in fast water – such as the tails of weirpools – is simply to trot through or spin slowly with a minnow attached to a size 10 hook. Chub will often take minnows fished in this fashion with little regard to presentation. As the season progresses, however, minnows lose their effectiveness owing to a preoccupation with anglers' baits and the fact that they become less numerous (the minnows, not the chub). One of the best

It looks bigger than its true weight of 5lb 1oz.

plugs to use must be the Heddon crazy crawler. This came to my attention when, after I had success on a red and white crawler for pike, a friend of mine got himself a black and green one. While I was doing well with the pike, he took only the odd one on this plug, but in three weeks of early morning fishing he did extremely well with the chub – six fish over 5lb, topped by an impressive chub of 6lb 5oz. The problem with fishing this particular lure, however, was that as it was a surface lure the chub tended to hit it anywhere. It was finally left in the box when one of the chub was hooked well outside its mouth and the flailing treble only just missed coming into contact with its eye. The problems mentioned above do not seem to occur when using subsurface lures. Incidentally, the red and white plug never took a chub. The Big S did produce a number of fish and although I have never taken a five-pounder on plug I personally do not feel that the risk of injury to the fish is worth taking by using surface plugs intentionally to catch them. Various plugs and spinners all have their day, and if all else fails it's a pleasant way to spend a few hours on the bank.

Fly fishing for chub is most definitely worth a try. When there is a good hatch of damselfly or if there are a good number of crane-fly about, the chub can become preoccupied, intercepting numbers of these as they are borne down by the stream. I have had a number of chub on fly during these times, and often carry a fly rod in the early part of the season just in case the opportunity arises. On some of the waters that I fish there is a fly-only rule anyway. These are obviously trout waters, and although I don't tend to fish them too often – especially if I have to pay for a ticket – it does make a pleasant change every now and again. The coarse fish in these sections are not caught all that often as the trout people have very little interest in things that they cannot eat. The coarse fish, therefore, have become large and these waters are well worth the occasional visit.

On certain stretches of the Stour that are very overgrown, chub respond well to floating crust. A typical approach is to arm yourself with a couple of large, uncut loaves and throw a few offerings into the head of a swim. It is simplicity itself to watch these pieces of bread make their way downstream until chub show themselves on the surface by sucking them in. All you need to do then is to float a piece of crust armed with a size 4 hook down to the chub and strike when one takes a bait. The chances of taking more than a couple of fish per swim are slim, so as soon as the fish stop showing move down river. Other chub will be all too ready to have a go at your bait, as the bits that are not taken in the swim that you have just left will soon be intercepted by others further down. A steady stream of chub can be had all the way down the stretch and you may well get an exceptional fish in this manner.

Line strength for these tactics needs to be around 4lb or so – providing there are not too many snags present. If there are snags then use 6lb line. Combine this with a soft rod of 1lb test, preferably ringed with the stand-off type used for float fishing, and a fixed-spool reel. The pin has no place in this type of fishing as the bread needs to be able to make its way unhindered by any pull from the reel, and casting to the far bank is much easier with the fixed spool. The tackle should be kept to an absolute minimum – rod, reel, landing net, forceps, a packet of size 4 hooks, and weighing and photographic gear is all that is required. When travelling this light it is quite possible to cover a great distance, so keep aware of the time should the water you are fishing be subject to leaving times.

Right, summer's over. There are no more grubs, all the slugs have died, and you have not seen a wasp for months. The river is up and coloured, it is freezing cold, and all the worms have emigrated to New Zealand. Now is the time for bread, pastes, cheese and meat baits, and big lumps of tinned meat. A mobile approach is the only way to fish for winter chub. Ledgering is the most successful and consistent way of sorting out the bigger fish, although trotting does have its day, and

A lovely 5lb 7oz Stour chub.

occasionally makes for a nice change. One useful tactic to employ is to drop a small amount of mashed bread in all the likely swims on the stretch you intend fishing. Then spend half an hour or so in each swim until you have covered the whole water.

Bear in mind that a lot of large chub in these conditions will not feed until it is nearly dark, so if the rules allow then aim to be on the water baiting up an hour or so before. If the rules do not allow this then it is up to you what you do! Do not just use bread in the baited swims – it is worth dropping a change bait in on the hook to try to produce a bite or two as this often works where bread has failed to get a pull. Alternatively, go straight in on pastes anyway. The variations on winter chubbing are many and what works one day will fail miserably the next. All you can do is keep ringing the changes until you catch fish.

During winter when the river is clear for any length of time, maggots are the bait to use, and lots of them - especially so when feeder fishing. When fishing the feeder for chub I use the fixed paternoster more than any other method. (From the amount of times the fixed paternoster gets a mention in this book you can rightly assume that this is a favourite rig of mine!) For the purposes of chub fishing it is fished on a longer tail than for any other species as chub have a habit of feeding at all depths. As the feeder hits the water on rivers such as the Hampshire Avon, it will start to empty immediately. The chub will often follow the feeder to the bottom a few feet behind it, taking the maggots as they drift downstream. Once the feeder has hit the bottom the bait will escape as intended and a tail of 6ft in length will allow any chub that is taking maggots 'on the drop' a chance to hook itself. The fact that chub feeding in this manner are moving all over the swim to intercept bait before it is swept away results in slam-around bites. These fish are usually hooked well into the back of the throat. If no bites occur as the feeder and hookbait settle on the bottom, most of the chub should now be at the back of the swim having followed the initial bait downstream. They will then start to move up again, following the stream of maggots coming from the feeder. Once the feeder has been in the water for as long as it takes to empty, it is time to recast and start again.

There are two methods of fishing the block-end feeder. Should you wish to fish with a bias toward the on-the-drop method, only fill the feeder to around half-full as this will ensure that most of the feed is out of it before it hits the bottom. Obviously, when fishing this method recasting will be far more frequent. If, on the other hand, you wish to get the fish hard on the bottom, cram as much bait into the feeder as possible. This method requires far less recasting – in steady water a 2oz feeder can be left for upwards of fifteen minutes before a refill is required. The amount of bait needed per rod for a day's fishing using either method is 3 pints or more. This can, of course, be supplemented with hempseed as, contrary to popular belief, it does work in winter!

Float fishing for chub with maggots can provide some very good results when conditions allow. Maggots will obviously catch many other species, but often chub will make an appearance in the swim sometime during the course of the day. When fishing with chub in mind, feed needs to be heavier than when fishing for other species such as roach. The 'little-and-often' principle needs to be modified to one of 'lots and often'!

It seems that chub are able to devour far more bait than any other fish that swims in Britain's rivers. The chub will move well up into the swim, arriving from great distances downstream once they get on the maggot trail. The problem is that these will be anything from tiny chub weighing mere ounces up to specimen size, the latter being hard to catch. They can also be extremely adept in crushing your bait without the merest hint of a bite – no other fish is as accomplished at this than the chub. Should you experience this then you must watch your float for any change in pace or direction. Anything that looks remotely like a bite has to be hit as although it often is not, it does happen. For most of the time chub are not this finicky and bites will be bold, with the fish taking the float well under and keeping it there. If, however, you are getting crushed maggots and no fish even when hitting bites on time, don't blame the dace as the chances are that the larger chub will be the culprits.

Stillwater Chub

Chub in stillwaters are a totally different kettle of fish, and only in recent years has the potential of these fish been realized. Primarily thought of as a river fish, the chub seems to thrive in all manner of pits, either connected to a river system or not. A lot of pioneering has been done using dead fish on larger gravel pits by such anglers as Peter Stone and others, with some excellent results to show for their efforts. My own stillwater chub experiences, however, have been restricted to somewhat smaller waters where often the chub have been visible both on the surface and whilst feeding off the bottom. One lake that I used to fish that springs to mind is one that is controlled by Wimborne and

District Angling Club, a secluded 2-acre lake fed by a small chalk-stream. In general, the lake is shallow with a maximum depth of around 5ft. During the summer months the water has a tinge of colour due to the abundance of small carp that it holds, but in winter the water is often gin-clear during prolonged cold spells when these carp are not so inclined to feed – and, of course, there are fewer anglers on the water.

During the summer months the chub can be seen cruising around on the surface, patrolling the margins and the island. One of the favourite methods employed by those after the carp on this water is floater fishing. The carp at the lake were suckers for anything and numbers could be taken in the space of a few hours – it was the sort of water to which you take a newcomer to the sport in full knowledge that the most incompetent of anglers cannot fail to catch!

The chub also became accustomed to the floating baits and ate them with abandon – unless they were attached to tackle! They proved near impossible to catch, but I only say near impossible as a young lad took the best fish and club record at an impressive 6lb 2oz on a strawberry jam flavoured dog biscuit! Most of the time the chub would come up to a floating bait, whether it be bread, dog biscuit or whatever, and take it beneath the surface by just holding it between its lips. Result: one missed fish on the strike. The bait would then float to the surface and the chub was provided with a free meal. This meant that few fish were actually caught on the floating offerings. I used various methods to try to overcome the problems involved in getting a fish on the bank, including fishing the hair rig in conjunction with hard, non-soaked dog biscuits. This worked for a while and the odd 4lb or 5lb fish did come to the bank, but again they soon wised up to what was going on.

Probably the best method anglers at the lake evolved was to make use of the overhanging bushes on the island. These bushes were in fact very sparse in terms of foliage but the chub, being far more wary of the bait than the demonically minded carp, would not venture too far from the cover they provided. It became standard practice to cast the bait into the bushes and then allow it to drop down on to the surface of the water. This achieved two things. First, as a carp approached you could pull the floater from the water away from it – this caused endless amounts of frivolous behaviour, as you can imagine. Second, when a chub took the bait you could convince it into thinking that it had got itself a free meal by pulling the bait out of its mouth and back on to the surface. As the chub had played that game before, it would come back up to take the bait and this time close its mouth. Using 6lb line it was easy both to strike the hook home and clear, or cut through the bush in one movement. Two contributing factors stopped the effectiveness of this method: to a lesser degree the chub started to wise up to this method; and, more significantly, the bushes became increasingly thinner in a very short space of time!

Winter fishing on this water caused far fewer problems. The chub spent their time patrolling either the island or the area at the top of the water where the stream came in. The best method once again was fixed paternoster maggots. The swim at the top of the lake was always a favourite as because it was narrow, visibility was often good due to the clarity of the water coming in from the chalk-stream. The method I used was to throw around 2 pints of white maggots into the swim, and then sit and wait for the fish to arrive. Chub would start to arrive in dribs and drabs for a while, staying in the swim for a short period before moving out again. This would go on for some time with more fish appearing on each visit. Eventually, the larger fish would show and I would start to fish. At the time when I used to fish the lake, the chub were mostly over 4lb – in fact, only two fish under 4lb had ever been caught. One was an obliging 3lb fish that seemed to be caught by everyone who fished for chub, and the other was a fish of a mere 2½lb that made the occasional appearance. Five-pound fish on the other hand were plentiful and reasonably obliging. In all, during the course of one season, the 6lb fish mentioned earlier was the best fish while 5lb 9oz was the next down – in fact, three different chub of this weight came out. There followed a number of lesser fives and a few, though not as many, fours. Sadly, the larger fish seem to have disappeared from the lake and, with no small fish to come through, it is no longer a viable chub water.

Other waters in the Avon valley in particular, and the Stour, hold numbers of large chub, but although the odd fish does come out on occasion, these are few and far between. In recent years whilst eel fishing I have experienced a lot of extremely fast runs when using deadbaits on one water. There are a number of chub in this water that have sometimes shown themselves to the carp boys who fish the lake on boilies. I have had upward of twenty runs in a night which have been not been hit, and I suspect that at least some of these were due to chub. Often the rig came back minus bait or, if I was using whole fish, half the bait was neatly chopped from the hook. I tried using heavy Kryston in an attempt to present the bait in better fashion with both eels and chub in mind, but as this cost me a personal best eel I have now gone back to wire. The screaming runs still occur on occasion and I am sure that most can now be attributed to the chub in this water. You would think that they would come out on conventional baits, but they don't – strange fish, these gravel pit chub.

To most anglers the chub is not regarded as a predatory fish. I will now relate a true story that I would have been inclined to disbelieve had I not seen it myself.

A friend of mine who is into keeping tropical and cold-water fish caught a few inch-long chub, using one of those small nets that children are often seen with in the shallows of rivers. He introduced these chub into one of his larger tropical community tanks where the fish in the tank were of similar size and above. All went well apart from the fact that he lost four chub in the first three days from the original twelve that he had put into the tank – over a period of a month or so the chub grew to about twice their original size.

I happened to be in his house one day when a consignment of neon tetras arrived. As these were destined for the same tank as the chub, a polythene bag was floated in the top of the tank to allow the temperature to stabilize. With the other resident fish in the tank having a good look at the new arrivals, little attention was paid to the chub. Once the bag was opened and the twenty-four neons were allowed to swim into their new home, the chub went crazy. In what only amounted to seconds every chub in the tank had a neon's tail sticking from its mouth. The ensuing fracas was entertaining to say the least.

The chub made very short work of the first fish and were on the hunt for more. Neons were darting everywhere with chub chasing the poor, defenceless fish in all directions. A net was quickly brought into play, however, and the remaining neons were removed to another tank – all seven of them! The chub had taken the rest. The chub were then caught and placed into another tank of their own. They are still alive and happy now in a 4ft tank and are fed a staple diet of guppies! So there you have it, predators from 2in long!

If it is accepted that a lot of the chub in our waters are to at least some extent predatory, then it is reasonably safe to assume that at least some of them are likely to be mainly predators. Knowing the way that chub feed, it is not surprising that few of the larger fish – in both rivers and stillwaters – are not often caught.

I have one last point to make with chub – photographs! I do not know the answer to this problem, but chub must be the most difficult of our coarse fish to capture on film. Although a 7lb fish will usually speak for itself if it is long, if it is rather short but with an immense girth this is not so apparent. It can be even more difficult in the hours of darkness to get a true representation of this sort of fish as the tail tends to disappear from the resulting shot. Conversely, a fish of only 4lb can appear to weigh in excess of 6lb – as in John Medlow's photograph.

All this makes you wonder just how many of the photographs of fish submitted to the angling press are actually truthful. The financial rewards that can be gained by adding a couple of pounds to the weight if the photograph looks the part are temptation enough for some. At the end of the day, however, the angler concerned would have to live with his or her own conscience, and should also realize that someone who has taken the genuine fish may well be stopped on a particular week from gaining their rightful place in the frame. This practice is not just confined to chub, but occurs with all species of fish. Some of these 'forgeries' are blatantly obvious yet the people concerned still collect considerable sums of money and some free tackle. The one thing they do not get, however, is the respect of other anglers, and eventually they will be found out. I look forward to the day that any such person is exposed, whoever they may be.

The fact is that there will always be those who cheat. In most sports proof is easy to obtain with the use of drug tests and so on, but in the case of angling it is far more difficult to prove that someone is cheating. Not a nice way to end a chapter, but I thought it needed to be said!

John Medlow with a chub you could put any weight you fancied to.
True weight 4lb 14oz.

5

Perch

Everyone must have caught a perch or two very early on in their fishing careers. Nearly every water held them in vast quantities, from small fish, average fish of an ounce or so to the leviathans of some waters weighing 4lb or more. The fish that I caught most in my youth were the former type, and only occasionally would I manage to get a fish weighing over a pound. This was mainly due to the fact that I did not understand what these larger fish ate.

As a teenager, the method I used for perch was float-fished worm, the brandlings I got from my grandfather's compost being most effective. I caught lots of perch, and although I could see the bigger fish I could never manage to get the bait through to them quickly enough. The small fish always seemed to get there first. Today, this is not so much of a problem as few waters hold any large stocks of perch. I know that in certain areas of Britain the perch do not seem to have suffered as much as they have in others, but in the Wessex area perch waters are now few and far between.

It was not until some years after these early experiences that I became aware that perch weighing over a pound or so are mainly predatory. I had seen lots of big perch on my travels, and I wish I had known then what I know now! Perch were a lot more prolific in the 1960s than they are today, but that is not to say that large fish do not get caught on other baits. On 4 March 1984, the perch record of 4lb 12oz was broken twice: first by Bill Weatherhead at a weight of 4lb 14oz from Jubilee Pool in Worcestershire; second by Ethel Owen, weighing in at 4lb 14oz 12dr from King's Lake in Hampshire. These fish were taken respectively on maggots and, would you believe it, floating crust!

Towards the end of the 1991–2 season, a fish of 4lb 12oz was taken from a small New Forest pond by an angler pole fishing with a double red pinkie. This pond is not known for perch at all and very few have ever been caught – but then again, no one to date has fished it seriously for perch. Maybe it will attract a certain amount of anglers who are prepared to try and tap the potential, but this will be hard as livebaits are banned on this particular water. As it is overrun with small fish, perhaps the best form of attack will be to use plugs and spinners. There are a lot of small ponds in the New Forest and this one, should you know where it is, would be the obvious place to start. But what of the others? If this one holds good perch then there must be a chance that at least some of the others do. With perch being scarce, any such reports are worth following up and expanding upon.

In the mid-1980s I had a go at beating my personal best fish of 2½lb. Armed with the knowledge that larger fish were predators, and having been informed of a good perch water, I set off to 'do the business' in late autumn. Hucklesbrook main lake was the venue, and being primarily a trout fishery, the potential of this water had never been over-exploited. My information was based purely on the results of a few matches over the previous years when coarse fishing had been allowed, and on reports of trout anglers taking large fish on lures. After spending two full days livebaiting, during which time I caught quite a few brown and rainbow trout, the owner made an appearance at the lake to collect the day ticket fee. Seeing the livebaits, he inquired

*A magnificent, bristling
2lb 9oz perch.*

as to what I was fishing for and, upon being told I was after perch, he
came out with some catastrophic news.

The perch in the water had apparently died the season before. He
informed me that the amount of large perch that had perished was
extremely high – dustbins full of them and weighing 5lb or more in
weight. They had started to turn up dead in the margins during the
middle of the closed season, first in small numbers and then as much
as four bin-loads a day for two weeks. Perch from mere ounces
through to the large fish all perished and were all buried. Some small
fish do still appear in this water from time to time, but they never seem
to reach any size. There must be adult fish left for the fry to appear in
the first place, but they do not seem to be able to acquire any immu-
nity to the disease.

My information was over two years old by then, and as I had been
out of the area for about a year I had not been around when this loss
had occurred and therefore knew nothing of it. Thwarted in my quest,
unhappily I started to pack up. The owner was very generous after our
long talk, and refused to take the money for the day ticket. He allowed
me to try the small lake as well, as some perch had been transferred

before the disease struck, and this was some consolation at least. After an hour or so on this lake without even a single sign of a fish, I decided that enough was enough and that these would probably be dead anyway, so I left.

A couple of years after this episode, news of another lake in the area came my way. It had started to show up the odd big perch, including fish to over 4lb. These fish had originally been transferred from another pond in the area that contained a large head of small fish with very few over a pound in weight. The fish in this small pond still all appear to be in perfect health but for some reason do not grow large, although the number of resident pike in this water may be a contributing factor.

It was not long after I heard this news that I was on the banks of this new (to me, anyway) water in search of these fellows. The general method used on this lake was somewhat unusual. With a keep net ban in force and an abundance of small fish, the practising match anglers (who were many) dropped their catch into the edge one by one. It did not take the perch long to capitalize on this, and as soon as any angler started to catch fish regularly, the big perch would move in and wait for fish to be dropped in. The top of the lake consisted mostly of undercut banks heavy with marginal rushes and a few dense lily beds, which made it easy for the big perch to lie in wait and ambush these free offerings.

On my first visit to the water I caught a 4lb 1oz perch, and it was easy! I had spoken to an angler who was snatching bits on a pole, and observed a big perch chasing the odd fish from its ambush point under the bank. I chose a swim about 20yd from the angler which had a lot of marginal weeds and an undercut bank. I started out by catching bits on a float rod, and dropped these very close to the bank after having retained the first two in a bucket. I waited until a big perch moved in and then I dropped a small roach – complete with size 4 hook tied direct to 4lb line – on its nose. The roach was taken straight away and I pulled the hook home. The resulting fight was exciting, to say the least, with the fish spending most of the time on the surface pulling all the way to the net. I had never seen a big perch at close quarters before, and it certainly made an impressive sight with the dark bars and brilliant red fins. During the season I took another 4lb fish, plus a few threes and lots of twos from this water.

Being able to observe perch at such close quarters gives a good understanding of their behaviour when they take fish. The perch I saw at this water would only chase a fish for a very short distance before

No wonder the author looks pleased with this beautiful fish, an ounce over 4lb.

giving up. The take consisted of completely engulfing the fish by sucking it in from a distance of about 6in or so. This would be from any direction; there was no preference shown for head or tail first. Most takes were from behind as the bait fish tried to escape, but if it changed direction at the last moment it made no difference to the perch. Unlike pike, which will invariably hit a bait and then turn it, perch take a fish whatever way it is facing.

If anything seemed wrong, the bait would be ejected immediately. If this happened the bait fish would often have been denuded of the majority of its scales, and though still alive and perfectly able to swim, any fish rejected in this way would then be ignored. A new bait would, however, be taken without any hesitation, so perch must be able to distinguish between a fish that has been rejected and a fresh bait. I would like to suggest that perch must have extremely good eyesight to be able to do this, and more so than any other predator – with the exception of zander, but these are known to attack and kill fish, coming back later to eat them.

Perch seem to be intolerant of any resistance. With that in mind, most of my perch fishing is done free lined. Even when I cannot see fish I tend to allow the bait fish to roam while I feel for takes by holding the line lightly. The take is usually preceded by the bait fish speeding up or suddenly changing direction. At this point I will release the line momentarily, then pull tight to see if the bait has been taken. When using a float in order to fish at longer range, I will always use one that affords little resistance to a taking fish. An alternative is to use the sunken polyball method as described in Chapter 1.

On the subject of livebaiting for perch, the question of when to strike after a take arises. Personally, I strike as soon as a take is evident. Although some fish are missed on the strike using this method, I would rather miss the odd fish than risk waiting for any length of time. A lot of anglers disagree with this and suggest you wait for ten seconds or more. If the reason for this is that the bait you choose to use is too big for the perch to engulf in one hit, then this is fine. But would it not just be simpler to use a smaller bait?

The argument that big fish require big baits does not hold up with perch. In fact, whilst observing the perch at close quarters in visible lakes, most bait fish over 4in long were usually ignored. To overcome the problems of fishing a larger bait, or to decrease the chances of missing a take, some anglers I know use two single hooks in tandem whilst perch fishing, one being mounted in or near the mouth of the bait fish and the other in the tail root. This method is fine, providing that nothing distracts you from missing the initial take – if a take is not noticed immediately two hooks can prove rather difficult to remove, and there is not an awful lot of room in the mouth of even the largest perch.

Hooks for livebaiting should be between a size 8 and size 4. Only single hooks should be used as a perch will often take a bait right down its throat in a matter of seconds . . . hence the need for an early strike! The structure of a perch is such that its vital organs are located immediately at the back of its throat, where the removal of any other hook could result in its death. Indeed, great care should be taken when removing single hooks and it is worth considering using barbless or microbarbed hooks. The one problem I have encountered when using single hooks is that sometimes the hook point becomes masked as the bait fish slides down the shank and, in the case of barbless hooks, it is impossible to keep the bait on for any length of time. One possible solution to this problem could be to use a double hook – this would leave one side completely clear to hook the perch. I have discounted this, however, as such a hook could once again prove difficult to remove without the risk of fatality.

Just look at that fin.

With multiple-hook rigs – including double hooks – banned on the water I was fishing anyway, I had to find an answer to this problem. It was temporarily overcome by using a small section of elastic band pushed up the hook shank after the bait to hold it in place. After a fashion, this was reasonably successful, but to be quite honest it was not the answer for me. Being lazy, I wanted something that I did not need to play around with. A few words with Alan Bramley of Partridge Hooks, to ask if a modification to a present hook could be made, solved my problems. Within a week a few packets of size 8, size 6 and size 4 Jack Hilton Carp Hooks dropped through my letter-box. These each had a neat little slice half-way up the back of the shank, similar to those in the worm hooks that one associates with sea fishing. There would be no more messing around with elastic bands for me!

The most effective bait fish without a doubt has got to be a small perch, around 2–3in long. I have reached this conclusion from my experiences over the last few seasons. I have found that other species such as roach or rudd tend to move away from snags and undercut banks. Although perch do, on occasion, seem to enjoy chasing and harrying fish, grabbing at their tails to slow them down before finally taking them (note yet another reason for using small baits – larger fish will very often outrun the perch!), this is rare. As small perch do not head for the open but are more likely instinctively to head for cover, they will hopefully swim straight into the waiting mouths of mum and dad!

On odd occasions perch can be seen attacking shoals of small fish. This provides a very impressive sight as they will be working as a pack. The shoals of bait fish are herded into a bay and the perch seem to take it in turns to surge into them while the others keep them penned in. Such occasions are rare but very obvious – the perch will be sending small fish in all directions as they surge through the shoals, and fish will be seen leaping out of the water in an attempt to escape. The large perch will show themselves at these times by bristling through the bait fish, fins erect and displaying their aggressive nature. A livebait cast into the middle of the shoal of fish will often provoke a take instantly, and during the time when the perch are actively feeding it is possible to take quite a good bag of fish. Small mepps-type spinners and plugs will also take fish at this time should you not be in possession of any suitable bait fish.

In the winter months when it is cold, the perch seem less inclined to take live fish. This is possibly due to decreased levels of activity of the smaller bait-sized fish, and the fact that they will have been severely

This magnificent 4lb 3oz perch fell to a plug.

depleted in number by the time winter arrives. The method to use at this time is lobworm, fished close into the bank or toward any remaining weed-beds or other cover the lake provides. Use either the float rod or ledger rod, but again bear in mind that minimum resistance is of paramount importance. This method has, however, proved a bit hit and miss and I have not had too much success with it. I have caught a few 2lb fish, but that is about as far as it goes. Others fared slightly better on the same water with the odd 3lb fish, but as far as I know only fish over 4lb came out to worm during this time. I was looking forward to the next season when the perch once again would be more responsive to fish baits when at the AGM in the closed season some bright spark decided to put in a proposal that livebaiting on this water be banned.

With very few big-fish men attending the meeting, the motion for this ban was carried easily. We were all extremely miffed to say the least that the 'only' method for catching these specimen fish had been taken from us. Still, that is what you get for apathy. At the next AGM, however, we went 'mob-handed'. I went through the rule book and found eight rules, including the one banning livebaits, that I and most other like-minded anglers would like changed. This included one on salmon, thrown in on the request of some anglers from the game side who agreed on principle with what we were attempting to achieve. Surprisingly, they were all carried.

During the season that we could not use livebait I fished the odd day there with plugs. I found the most effective to be a perch pattern kwik-fish, and the slower I retrieved the lure the better. Often I would feel the perch knocking at the back of the lure a few times before it developed into a positive take. I was lucky enough to hook and land a new and still personal best of 4lb 3oz whilst using this method, but the perch soon became wise to plastic and refused to take. I would get the odd knock or two but these never seemed to develop into proper takes.

For a change of tactics, I tried using baited spinners with some success. Various bits of fish, worms and the mepps-bar-type spinners with dyed wool woven around the hook were successful for a while, but soon these, too, became ineffective. The trouble with this method is that it is totally non-selective – fish of all sizes took the various offerings, including perch not much bigger than the lures themselves. At what stage in their life do they become predators? It seems to be not long after they reach a few ounces in weight.

The funniest day of the season was provided when one of the gentlemen who had originally instigated the livebait ban challenged me for using plugs and spinners. I think he was slightly put out by the fact that there were moves afoot to overturn the ruling at the next AGM and by the fact that I was catching perch by lure fishing. The water on the day was packed. 'Can't use spinners or plugs here!' he bellowed across the lake. I totally ignored him. He came round to my side of the lake, during which time I had hooked and landed another perch of a pound or so, returned it and carried on with my fishing.

'I'm going to report you to the committee for using spinners,' he informed me.

'It's not against the rules,' I countered.

'Oh yes it is. There are no trebles allowed on here.'

It was with great pleasure that I reeled in to hold the plug I was using under his nose. The treble had been replaced with a size 4 single hook and not a word needed to be said. He seemed somewhat confused on the way back round the lake! I hasten to add here that he was a match angler and was totally against the specialists in the club.

During this same season the fish started to develop some nasty sores on their flanks. I had seen this before on a lake in Wilmslow during the mid-1960s when I lived in Manchester and therefore I knew that the days of the perch were now numbered. Sure enough, the first fatalities started to show late that season. The anti-livebait brigade in the club tried to lay the blame on the perch anglers for the loss, saying that we were still using live fish. Would you believe that the logic they based this argument on was that if a perch does not have the bait fish removed from its throat that it is likely to choke to death, or at least have difficulty in breathing for some time until it can eject the bait? Obviously well-informed anglers! They were then told of the dreaded perch disease by those that knew. It never ceases to amaze me just how stupid various factions of anglers can be when they do not agree with something another faction does. As anglers, we should all be fighting for each other against our common rivals and not forming groups to interfere with each other. Who needs the anti-angling brigade when there seem to be more than enough adversaries amongst our own ranks?

The next year big perch were not so plentiful, and toward the middle of the season most had perished. The year that the livebait ban was in force was probably the time when these fish were at their peak. The present club record on this water stands at 4lb 12oz, taken by an angler using sweetcorn during the year of the livebait ban. This was by no means the largest fish in the water at the time and there was one particular fish that quite a few anglers who knew what they were looking at reckoned to be easily over 5lb. Now we will have to wait and see if the fish remaining after the disease has run its course manage to attain the weight of their predecessors. Previous lakes which the disease has decimated show this to be unlikely, but perhaps this one will prove different.

Another lake in the area also produced the odd big fish. A few fish over 4lb were caught in the same season, but then these, too, started to decline. It seems that perch get to their peak, quickly succumb to the ravages of the disease and die. There still appears to be no evidence – apart from that which is circumstantial – to suggest the method by which disease is transferred from one water to another, if indeed it is. Apparently, the *aeromomas* bacteria which causes the disease is present at all times, but this does not really seem to ring true, as if it were the case then even the small farm ponds described in the next paragraph would surely suffer. Something must actually trigger an outbreak of this disease, but no one has yet established what it is. Sometime there may be a plausible answer and solution to the perch problem, but until that day we have to accept that they will die *en masse*.

The disease is a fact of life, or should I say death, with perch. The only waters that seem to escape it are isolated small ponds that do not offer good flight paths for visiting birds. Jim Gibbinson puts this theory forward in his chapter in the book *Modern Specimen Hunting*. Whilst he based his study mainly on the perch in the Kent area and this one is based on the Wessex area, the generalization is much the same. When I lived in Manchester there were, as far as I know, only two waters to escape the disease. One of these was a small farm pond surrounded by trees, and the other was a small, disused stone quarry surrounded on three sides by sheer 20ft-high walls and on the remaining side by large trees. Both of these waters were miles from any others and the only birds to inhabit them were the odd pair of resident moorhens.

If big perch do show in any water that does not fit the aforementioned type, make sure you get there soon and catch some as they will not be there for long!

River Perch

All the previous text is related to stillwaters, but what of rivers? Most of the rivers in the Wessex area contain a number of resident perch. Chalk-streams such as the Hampshire Avon and the Nadder contain some very good fish (as did the ill-fated Allen). These perch are often in excess of 2lb with the occasional fish reaching 3–4lb but very few of these fish actually get caught. With the majority of anglers fishing for other species on the main rivers, any that do get caught are usually flukes.

Perch on the upper Avon once existed in relatively high numbers, and shoals – particularly in and around the Salisbury area – were often spotted during the mid-1980s. Some of the fish in these shoals were in excess of 4lb, and I once came across such a shoal consisting of around twenty fish with a few estimated to eclipse this weight.

Once again, however, this was before I realized that perch were mainly predators, so livebait was not a method I used. With the water of the Avon gin-clear, I actually watched the fish take the offerings of a float-fished worm, striking when they engulfed the bait. The largest fish that I took in the few days that they were in this particular swim was just a shade over 2lb. Not once did any of the exceptionally large fish show any interest in the worm, but one thing that did become apparent was that the ones that did certainly had never read any of the Mr Crabtree books. The characteristic take described, with the float bobbing as the perch takes the bait and blows it out again, just did not happen – at least not in the context that the book demonstrates. The

A quite superb 4lb 2oz perch.

fish would take the worm and keep it, providing that nothing felt wrong. If a bait was ejected, the perch responsible would not take it for a second time, but another fish in the shoal would soon be upon it. This scenario occurred more than once within the shoal of fish.

The actual way a fish takes the worm, however, is very much the same as described by the book. The perch approaches a bait, and from a distance of a few inches, flares its gills and sucks the bait in from this position. This, in effect, creates a vortex of water in which the bait is contained. This volume of water and bait is then taken into the mouth, and if any resistance or other unnatural behaviour is detected, the bait is ejected in the reverse manner. This is synonymous with the action of the float described by the author. With the modern polarizing glasses that we have today, we have an advantage over Mr Venables – if we were limited in the same way as he was at that time, no doubt we would come to the same or very similar conclusions.

The River Itchen, on which I did most of my apprenticeship, held some enormous perch in its middle reaches at the time. I was often in the habit of wandering the banks in search of trout, armed with a seven-piece spinning-type rod which could be hidden quite nicely under my waterproof coat. Yes, I was poaching – or as I like to call it, guesting. As I was only very young at that time, the worst that could have happened to me was the odd clip around the ear – that is assuming the water-keeper was quick enough to catch me once I had taken to my heels. In those days I considered this an acceptable risk, but would not have dreamed of telling my parents about it as no doubt I would have received another! I feel sorry for the water-keepers of today, as by law they have to punish any such action by prosecution.

I took great delight in escaping the water-keeper on this water on many occasions in my youth. The nearest I got to being caught was when guesting during the hours of darkness. The first I knew of the keeper's presence was when the heavy hand of authority fell on my shoulder while I was fishing a weirpool. The artful dodger in me soon saw me shrugging off his hold, and I made my way across the fields at high speed with the keeper, as they say, in hot pursuit. Neither of us could see ahead of us the freshly seeded cricket pitch which was surrounded by a single wire at knee-height. I was at least 30yd in front of the water-keeper when I hit it. I ended up face-down in the dirt, but picked myself up only to hurtle straight into the wire on the other side of the pitch. As I got up for a second time I heard my pursuer curse as he tripped over the first wire. As I reached the safety of the road and jumped onto a passing bus, I could just make him out half-way between the second wire and the road. There would be no more guest-ing at night for me!

Anyway, to get back to the point, the perch I saw on this stretch of the Itchen were in an area half a mile above the weir. This was at a point where a weed boom lay (and perhaps still lies), and the banks on both sides are endowed with very large willows to which the boom itself was attached. The force of the current had scoured out a deep hole in the river bed just below the boom, and had also created two eddies on the banks immediately above and below it. Perch could be seen swimming at mid-depth, passing under the boom and the cover it afforded into both of the eddies. While my judgement at the time may have been on the optimistic side owing to my youth, I now feel that these fish were of a similar size to the 4lb perch that I have taken since. Sadly, however, I could not fish at this point as it was clearly visible to the keeper should he approach from any direction.

I have often wanted to go back to this section of the river to see if my youthful estimations were correct, but with the advantage of being no more than a young child taken from me with the passing of time, I have had not had the opportunity to fish it. Until very recently it has been a rather exclusive dry-fly-only trout water, but news has recently filtered through to me that an angling club has now acquired the fishing rights on this water owing to diminishing returns on the trout fishing side. When I heard this information I found it hard to believe and made a few telephone enquiries. It has indeed proved to be correct, however, and coarse anglers are now allowed access from 1 October until the end of the season. Needless to say, I will find some time to investigate the potential of the water. If I do not find any perch I will know that the dreaded disease has struck once again.

It will certainly be an interesting exercise to fish this water as I have not even set eyes on it since the age of about thirteen. I wonder just how many changes in the quality of the fishing and in the water itself will be evident. Such changes are not as noticeable when you fish a water on a regular basis as when you see one after a considerable break, and I do hope that my expectations are at least in part realized. At the time of writing, the 1992–3 season is only just around the cor-ner and I will soon be able to find out. Feelings of euphoria and trepi-dation are running simultaneously as in my mind's eye I remember what the river once was.

The author with a beautiful river carp of 18lb 6oz.

*Don't you wish they would all put their fins
up! A 9lb 9oz Hampshire Avon fish.*

*Cary Culverhouse with his first
Avon fish of 10lb 3oz.*

The author's best chub; a short, fat 5lb 10oz
upper Avon fish.

A very deep 5lb 6oz chub.

Four fish in four casts; three doubles and a twenty.

Mark 'Big Nose' Hateley with his example of Esox.

A lean, mean pike of 20lb 4oz.

The author's best river roach of 3lb 5oz.

A lovely night-caught fish of 2lb 12oz from the Stour.

A typical grayling pool on the River Itchen.

The author with his record 3lb 12oz grayling.

A wild brown trout of 6lb 10oz from the River Stour.

6

Pike

Pike are not the savage creatures that certain factions amongst our ranks would have us believe. I have heard it said by more than one fishery bailiff that the only good pike is a dead one. This is not the case.

Pike have a particular ecological role to play in Britain's waters. The main advantages for their presence are that they thin out sick and ailing fish, and that they provide a balance of fish of all sizes to interest the pleasure angler and big-fish man alike. As an illustration of this, I would like to use a particular fishery on the Dorset Stour as an example. This 2-mile stretch is above Blandford, and its control is divided inasmuch as one bank is controlled by Ringwood Angling Club and the other by Durwestern.

During the early 1980s when I lived in Blandford this was a very balanced fishery with some good roach up to over 2lb in weight, along

The author with a fabulous Avon pike at 27lb 13oz.

with a fair amount of chub approaching 5lb. Although the pike present were not monsters, the odd one did attain just over 20lb and there were a few high doubles.

In 1982 a new bailiff took over the Durwestern side of the fishery. Unfortunately, he fitted my earlier description of a pike-hating bailiff, and during the next two winters all the large pike were wiped out. Attacks on keep nets and on taken fish on their way in ceased initially, but although subsequent seasons saw an increase in the amount of fish other than pike caught, there was a decline in the individual average weight of the fish. Then the jack explosion occurred.

As there were no big pike left to give the jacks a hard time, they thrived. A lot of small food fish support a lot of jacks, and with the majority of the pike growing at the same rate, they progressed to 10lb or so in a short space of time. Then, of course, they were able to eat the larger prey fish, the result being that the fishery was out of balance and with the increase in pike numbers, other fish stocks declined. The pike then also declined through a lack of prey fish, although when I say that they declined, in reality they moved to pastures new. Today, ten years on, the fishery is at last showing signs of its former glory with fish of all sizes present again. What a waste of ten years!

Another way that a pike water can be destroyed in a very short space of time is when a lightly fished water suddenly becomes more accessible. A classic example of this is again on the Stour.

23lb 10oz of well-conditioned Stour pike.

In the 1986–7 season I found a very good pike water. It was little fished as the best pike section of the fishery was a good mile from the nearest access point from either bank. The only other person I ever saw piking there was Mark Vials and, although nothing was pre-arranged, we always fished opposite banks. In the course of that season I caught a lot of high doubles and five different fish of over 20lb, including my best at 30lb 12oz. The next fish down on this list weighed 28lb 4oz, so you can see this was a very good pike water. The length of the section was around a mile and lay between two weirs, so obviously the food fish population in this area was extremely high. Along with the usual fish found on the Stour, this section also had a large stock of sizeable bream. Big shoals of bream equal good pike fodder!

The next season I caught another two different 20lb fish to add to my list of successes. Mark also did well, catching two twenties and a number of high doubles. It was also during this period that a fish of 28lb 12oz met an untimely end at the hand of a pike-hater – perhaps the fish that I took at a similar weight around the same time. I would think that it is safe to assume that there were in the region of ten or more fish of over 20lb, along with a lot of back-up doubles.

It was then that the controlling club negotiated a new access point. The car-parking area was right on the bank next to one of the hot spots and less than a hundred yards from the other. It was not long before a decent pike was caught, the first out being the thirty-pounder which weighed 32lb 8oz this time. A week later it was out again to the same angler at 33lb 1oz. Needless to say, the angler concerned was very pleased – too pleased in fact, as he told everyone exactly where he had caught the fish. The result was hordes of inexperienced pike anglers and lots of dead pike. One of the most distressing experiences of my fishing career was when I encountered a fish of 16lb 12oz that I had taken the previous season at 23lb 10oz. The fish was stitched up in the throat cavity with two trebles that were more suitable for plugs used for marlin. They were tied directly to monofilament line.

Although the fishery has not yet suffered unduly with the loss of small fish, the amount of small pike in the 2–5lb class is on the increase. Fortunately, some of the large fish are still there – as in 1991 one of my friends showed me a picture of a 28lb pike that was taken on meat when barbel fishing in the summer. Yes, you guessed it, the 30lb fish in summer condition! As Jim Gibbinson so rightly stated in his book, pike thrive on neglect and cannot survive the exploits of the inexperienced angler. Both Mark and I were amongst the first anglers to fish this water for pike and the results speak for themselves. There is no way that I would have mentioned this water had the pike still been a well-kept secret, as it certainly would not have taken an awful lot of work to track it down! Pike receive a lot of attention simply because their very size is of interest to so many.

The same fish at 16lb 12oz. Note the markings above the ventral fin.

River piking demands a lot of leg work in the capture of decent fish, for they are on the move constantly. A typical stretch of either the Avon or Stour will usually hold at least one fish over 20lb. Finding that fish, however, is a different story. The previously mentioned length is not typical of these rivers as most waters are fished on a regular basis. The fish become used to pressure and move around accordingly. Pike can often be spotted during the summer months in all manner of swims, a lot of which would normally be disregarded by most pike anglers. Often they will be in very fast water, particularly if good shoals of prey fish are in evidence. Once you have located these fish you should note their positions if you consider them worthy of attention in the winter months. You would expect the changes in the river once winter arrives to push the pike into slacker water. Although a lot of fish do follow the rules, as it were, an awful lot do not. The obvious pike swims, unless there is a great amount of walking to do, receive more than their fair share of attention. The pike become accustomed to seeing angler's tethered baits and, although they will hit them, the amount of dropped takes in these swims are high.

In the less obvious swims, dropped takes are rare. A big slack will receive lots of attention once pike fishing gets under way, but if you are the first to fish one of these in the season then you will almost certainly catch pike. Within a short space of time, however, the pike will use these swims as a resting place in between meals rather than as an ambush point. I once spent most of a morning in one such swim with both livebaits and deadbaits in front of a twenty-pounder's nose. The pike did show interest, and at one time it looked as if it was definitely going to have the livebait. It then moved off out of the swim into the main current. I could still see the fish as it moved off upstream and I overtook it on the bank, whereby my dace livebait was taken the first time it was dropped in!

The amount of time I now spend in these sort of swims is kept very short – no more than half an hour unless fish are being caught. Once ten minutes have elapsed since I caught the last fish, I am on the move again, although I may drop a bait into the swim later in the day in case a fish has moved in. There is no such thing as a pike swim on these rivers as the pike can and do turn up anywhere. Every now and again, however, one of the obvious swims turns up a lot of good fish in a very short space of time. Mark Vials had an excellent day's fishing on the Stour when he caught over 180lb of pike from a well-fished pike water. I myself did well the next month on the Avon with a similar weight of fish, but had the advantage that the stretch had not been pike fished extensively before. In this case the pike all came from 'obvious' swims. By the end of the season, however, these fish had received quite a lot of pressure in a short space of time and were happily dropping the baits.

Livebaiting

Livebaiting for river pike will outfish any other method. Don't get me wrong, river pike do take deadbaits but with these it is very much a waiting game – so much so, I find, that if I cannot use livebaits on rivers in the winter I don't fish them. The most easily caught baits for pike are dace. Prolific on both the Avon and Stour, the dace always provide me with plenty of bait for a day's fishing. I like my baits to be around 6–8oz in weight, and grade them as they are caught. Any that are too small are returned to the water immediately. All fish of the suitable weight will find their way into my keep net, and this is in fact the only time I tend to use a net to retain fish. The average size of Avon dace in particular is high, and often fish of around 1lb are caught – in the season of 1991–2, I took five dace of 1lb or over, which I also returned to the water. Roach and chub will also make useful livebait, and any under 1lb will find themselves used if dace are hard to come by on a particular day.

The ethics of using live fish for bait is an emotive one, but I personally see nothing wrong with it. If one wishes to argue that hooking a fish to use it as bait causes it pain, then we may as well join the anti-angling brigade and give up fishing! Pike are not the only species that take fish; every fish that swims eats fish. Many branches of our sport would therefore suffer should a national livebait ban come into force. I think that should this ever happen then a ban on fishing other than for the table would follow not long after – this is what happened in Germany.

Although fishing is allowed in Germany, the rules there are that anything caught must be killed as otherwise the fish would suffer. Failure to comply with this law leads to prosecution. Imagine having to knock a 40lb pike or double-figure barbel on the head just so you could continue fishing! Oh, and by the way, it does not stop there – these days most German anglers fish waters over the border in Holland or in other countries for fear of attack on the banks in their own country. Enough said!

Gravel pits and lakes seem to fish quite the opposite. Without a doubt, sea-fish baits and freshwater deads (either whole or as halves) will generally outfish livebait. All sea-fish are successful as bait, the most common being, not in any order or preference: herring, mackerel, sardine and sprat. While takes with deadbaits on rivers are obvious, they are not as conspicuous on the pits. When fishing livebait on pits the pike will hit the bait hard, often running with it. When picking up a deadbait, however, the take will be hard to notice, often no more than a couple of bleeps on the Optonic. Bite indication therefore has to be positive. The J. S. eel rig lends itself well to pike fishing as the pike will always pull the line through the Optonic.

Locating gravel pit pike is harder than river pike, and the only way that you will find them is to put the hours in. Do not neglect margin swims. Often the classic approach to pit pike is to get a rod that will punch a whole herring to the skyline and do just that with it. Most prey fish are found within the first 30yd of the bank – it stands to reason that the pike will be where the food is and not out in the middle of the pit in areas devoid of fish. Take note of swims that get pleasure fished a lot as these will provide a good place to start. It sound obvious doesn't it? Yet on one such pit, most anglers are still more impressed with the distance they can cast than the amount of fish they catch.

Just 3oz over the 20lb mark. Taken from the margins.

Pike fishing in recent years has received a most valuable boost. It started when the Welsh Water Authority opened Llandegfedd Reservoir over a two-week period one October for what they called an experiment in the pike fishing potential. The pike anglers of Britain were quick to book boats on this water but so too were certain trout fishermen. There were lots of objections from the trout anglers, and as a protest they booked boats that were then left idle on the banks. Nevertheless, most of the boats were still taken out as a combination of neglect and the diet of rainbow trout meant that anticipations were high. The best pike caught in this period weighed in at an impressive 44lb 7oz, taken by Carl Garrett. Other 40lb fish taken were Stuart Gilham's 44lb fish, Brian Ingram's 43lb 2oz fish and Pete Climo's 42lb 5oz specimen which at the time was the lure-caught record. There were also a fair number of back-up fish over the magic 30lb mark. I had three days on the water myself during the second week and blanked along with most of the others. Subsequently, a pike of 45lb 7oz was caught in March 1990 by Gareth Edwards on a Toby Lure, thereby taking both the lure-caught record and pike record at the same time. More recently, a fish of 46lb has been taken on a lure here.

Another reservoir, Bough Beech in Kent, opened its gates in the 1991–2 season to pike fishing. Again, the season's best pike from this water weighed 40lb 8oz, this time to Trevor Simpson. In years to come more trout waters may open up to pike fishing, and I am sure that it will happen as it will provide extra revenue at a time when most of the boats will otherwise remain idle. How long, I wonder, before the 50lb mark is beaten?

My Search For Pike

My first impression of pike was that they were a pain in the neck! They would annoy me intensely, especially when I was fishing for roach. On one occasion when I was roaching on a stillwater, a pike managed to wind me up so much that I put a small fish on for bait. The result was one pike of 18lb which I ate, as this was the done thing in Manchester.

That was back in 1971. These days I treat pike with a great deal of respect, but the way in which I really became interested in pike was a very slow process. I was still being pestered by pike on and off, but instead of killing them I would catch them and move them to another swim. Once I moved down from Manchester to the Wessex area and started fishing the rivers there, these attacks became more frequent.

The amount of pike in this area was far greater than the lakes of the north-west (probably because most of these were dead), and once you got a shoal of roach feeding the pike would soon move in. On most trips either my keep net would get savaged or a fish would get taken. I would use a small fish as bait, usually mounted on a single treble hook and wire trace, catch the pike and move it to another swim. This was very much in the region of opportunist piking, with the main priority being to get the said pike out of the way. This did not catch me any really big fish but I did catch a lot of pike into double figures.

It was not until the early 1980s that I started to fish for pike seriously, and then it was only by chance. I was heavily into barbel at the time, almost to the exclusion of all other species. One day in mid-November I got a phone call from Rob Castle in Salisbury. He was very excited at having landed his first 'twenty' from Peter's Finger Lake on the outskirts of the city. After he had calmed down a bit he asked how I was doing. My reply? 'Rubbish!' I had not had a barbel for six weeks.

The conversation then switched back to pike. Basically, he had loads of livebaits and I had access to Bickton on the Hampshire Avon. A deal was struck. He would supply the bait in exchange for a day's fishing (the syndicate allowed members to take a guest). It seemed a pretty fair deal to me, and as it had been freezing for the last month the chances of catching barbel were remote anyway. Thoughts of big pike crossed my mind and the tales of pike attacking little old ladies paddling in the river, eating dogs and dragging in unsuspecting horses complete with cart, along with all the other incredible stories came flooding back. I think the best one I ever read was an account from a German pike angler. Apparently his dog, a Jack Russell, was swimming in the lake when it was taken by a large predator. Not wishing to lose his dog, the angler went home and collected some tackle to which a herring was attached. The pike responsible for this despicable act weighed over 50lb when it was caught, and when its stomach was cut open his dog reputedly jumped out, none the worse for his experience. Fair enough, it was in the *Daily Sport* so perhaps it wasn't true. But then again, he could have said his dog was a German shepherd!

Rob and I arrived at the car-park at first light and made our way to the river. Rob knew where he wanted to fish and seemed to know more about this section than I did, so off we trudged through the mist to the Whirlypool. I then realized that I had no snap tackle, but ever-helpful Rob supplied the lot. Rob, the experienced pike angler, was to fish two rods, one on deadbait and one on livebait, while I just fished the one. I took my instructions from Rob and cast out the livebait. The float went under straight away and I struck, only to clean the hooks out of an overexuberant dace. Feeling a bit stupid, I put on another bait and recast.

Rob had his livebait rod out around 10yd away from mine and both floats were bobbing about to the movements of the baits. A second rod was baited with a herring and dropped in just off the edge by Rob, who then attempted to clip on a drop-back indicator. He did not actually have time to clip it on, but instead took the rod from the rest saying, 'I've got a take.'

This was amazing – he had only just dropped the bait in after all! He wound down and pulled into the fish. Off it shot across the current and then it took off out of the water, shaking its head in the air before crashing down again. I was impressed – the pike I had been catching on my roach fishing trips had not fought like this. It was brought under control quickly and landed safely. Once on the bank, the fish was taken from the landing net and rolled on to its back while Rob calmly inserted a finger into the back of its gill cover and deftly removed the hooks with the aid of forceps. The speed with which this was done was very impressive. The fish was then weighed and went 18lb 4oz. A few photos later it was back in the river.

Meanwhile the livebait rods were still out there without so much as a sniff. Rob recast the deadbait out a little further than last time and we settled down to await the results. After a good fifteen minutes my until-now-motionless float suddenly shot off to the left for about 3yd and sank out of sight. I picked up the rod, looked at Rob for instructions and was told to hit it. I did just that and the rod bent over as the hooks went home. A short, spectacular fight later it was in the net and on the bank. I then make a complete fool of myself trying to get the hooks out and was given an invaluable lesson on how to do it properly. Anyone who is about to take up piking would do well to go out with an experienced angler for a few trips just to learn how to do this. After all, it is pointless catching a fish and then realizing too late that you do not know how to deal with it once it is on the bank. The fish was weighed and went 13lb. Again, it was returned to the river after some photos were taken.

All told, we had fourteen fish that day. Only two were under 10lb, with Rob's first fish being the biggest. We packed up around 5 p.m., and I was thoroughly impressed with the day's sport.

Over the next week I spent a couple of evenings fishing for dace in readiness for the weekend. I had remembered seeing a big pike lower down on the Avon whilst barbel fishing the previous summer and had decided to have a go for it. I got on to the water at exactly 8 a.m. – the

A very nicely shaped and coloured 21lb 5oz fish.

earliest time you are allowed on this section – and made my way down to the swim some mile and a half from the car-park. Now there's a clue for location.

Once there I had a look around. The river was up a bit from the previous weekend, and was pushing hard through the main stream slightly too fast for holding a bait out in the current. About 20yd from where I had seen the pike there was a small carrier that was usually only about a foot deep. I went to have a look at it and found it well up and virtually still – a textbook pike swim if ever there was one!

Bringing the tackle down, I thought the chances were pretty good. I put on my biggest dace and dropped it into the edge of the carrier. The float settled at first but seconds later was dragged under. It remained clearly visible a foot under the surface and just sat there, and as I was not sure if it was a take or not I tightened down to check. As I wound down and lifted the rod I felt a pike move off towards the main river. I pulled the hooks in and the fish took off at speed, leaving a massive boil in its wake. It was clear that this was a pretty good fish as the rod had taken on an alarming curve and I was having to let the fish have its own way – unusual for me as I generally give a fish a lot of stick and can slow most of them down without too much trouble. This one was proving a bit more difficult, however, and continued to give me an extremely hard time.

On the first occasion I managed to get it near the bank it surged off again, but this time the run did not extend quite so far. I brought the fish back toward me and caught sight of it. It was immense and I had never seen a fish like it. Now I was worried. Would the line hold? Did I make up the snap tackle properly? I leaned into the fish and brought it to the net – in it went and the battle was over.

I removed the hooks, which were set neatly in the roof and corner of the mouth, and admired the fish. I slipped it into the keepsack and sat there for a few minutes taking it all in. I knew it was big and thought that it must be nearing 30lb. After collecting my shattered nerves I got the scales out and, full of anticipation, weighed the pike. The scales settled at 27lb 8oz, nearly 10lb heavier that my previous best! To say that I was pleased would be an understatement. After the photos were finished I released the pike and packed up. I had had enough excitement for one day and was back at the car before 10 a.m. I suppose I should really have continued, but after this fish anything else would have been an anticlimax. I was in a state of euphoria and was in no condition to continue fishing! That night it was my turn to phone Rob up and tell him the news. He was extremely pleased and congratulated me on my success.

The next weekend saw us both on the same section, and I invited Rob to have a go at the swim. He departed downstream and I went off upstream. About two hours later a soaking wet and broadly grinning Rob appeared. 'Got one. I had to go in for it!' he exclaimed. Apparently, it had gone into a snag and, being a complete lunatic, he had gone into the river to get it out. This fish turned out to weigh 18lb 4oz. After we had gone back to the swim and some photos were taken it was returned. I made my way back up river and continued fishing. Around an hour later Rob was back looking rather blue and announced he was off home as he was freezing cold. Well wouldn't you be if you had jumped into a river in the middle of winter when the remains of the night's frost were still on the ground?

The following week I decided to have another go at the carrier swim to see if I could catch the 18lb fish. The river was up even higher than on my last visit and I had to balance on the footbridge over the carrier to fish it. As I cast in, the dace livebait came straight back to the surface pursued by a very large pike. The pike took the bait almost at my feet, soaking me as it turned back round with the dace well inside its mouth. I pulled into the fish and set the hooks. The pike powered off toward the main river and I put on as much pressure as I dared. If the pike had made it to the river I am sure I would have had a difficult job in controlling it as the banks were underwater and not visible at the time. Luckily however, after a few surges around the edge of the flow it came back to the net and was landed safely. When I got the fish to the bank I recognized immediately that it was the same fish that I had caught before. When I weighed it this time it went to 28lb 2oz – a new personal best. The following day I caught the fish that Rob had caught, and at the same weight. This pike fishing is easy, I thought – two decent fish in less than a month. However, it was to take me over two years and a lot of hard work to get my next fish over 20lb.

With my respect for and interest in pike now firmly established, I looked forward to 1 October with anticipation. Would this season see a new personal best on the bank? For a couple of years all my pike fishing centred on the Hampshire Avon which at one time held the record, with a fish of 37lb 8oz taken in 1944 by C. Warwick. I believe that this fish was taken from the Fordingbridge area. I fished hard for pike for two seasons on the Avon, but although I was getting plenty of fish, twenty-pounders continued to avoid me like the plague!

At this time Broadlands Lake was very prominent in the angling press. I remember a report in 1986 covering two huge fish, one from Broadlands Lake (a fish of 39lb 4oz) and the other from the Royalty at 37lb 8oz. The report read something along the lines of: 'sure to be a record' and 'knocked on the head'. Lorrie Tyler was the captor of the Broadlands Lake fish and this was returned, but the other fish was

The 27lb fish had grown a bit to 28lb 2oz!

109

killed! Soon after this, Lorrie caught another high thirty pounder. As much as I did not like fishing stillwaters at the time, Broadlands seemed the place to be. I spent a couple of weeks on the lake fishing with sea-fish deadbait in the hope of taking a thirty pounder. Even a 20lb fish would have been nice, but I failed in my efforts. The best fish I got weighed 18lb. The rules of the fishery were restrictive in that the only bait allowed was either trout (which had to be purchased from the fishery) or sea baits. At the time I had confidence in neither; the trout livebaits available were far too small to offer much of a mouthful to any self-respecting pike, and I had caught few pike on sea-fish baits.

By mid-November I was back on the river. Having spent a considerable amount of time on the Avon without another decent fish to show for my efforts, I thought a change of river was in order. The Stour was the obvious choice. With no livebaits in readiness, I spent some time trying to catch a few roach. This was a double-edged affair using breadflake as I hoped I might catch a good roach as well as the livebait. It all proved to be a disaster – after three hours I had one roach in the sack, a fish around the 10oz mark.

I decided to have a go for the pike with my one bait. I fully expected that a small jack pike would soon have the bait and that would be the end of pike fishing for the day. Five swims later, I still had not had so much as a sign of a take. By now I was a good mile away from the access point and had passed two cobbled weirs. Then I came across *the* swim – real Mr Crabtree stuff. It screamed of pike and was the last in a series of tight bends with a back water meeting the outside edge.

I cast the bait out toward the point where the current met with the still water, and the roach belted back into the slack. As the depth here was no more than two feet, I felt that the float was a hindrance and removed it. Casting back to the same spot, the roach again tried to swim away into the slack. I applied some side-strain and slowed it down a bit. At this point the bait was hit, and an almighty boil erupted as a pike turned back toward the crease. The amount of water the fish moved indicated that it was a good fish, and I tightened down to feel which way the pike was facing. As I did so the fish moved off slowly. I leaned into it and the rod went over as the hooks took hold. Once it realized it was hooked, it belted off toward the edge of the fast water. I piled on the pressure and turned it back to the slack, and as it returned it was visible just beneath the surface. This was a big pike and, as it made its way along the far edge of the slack, I realized that this was the thirty-pounder I was after.

I leaned into the fish, took control and brought it over the net. With no drama and no attempt to surge away for a second time, the fish slipped over the rim and was netted on the first try. As I put it on to the scales, the dial went round to settle at my personal record weight of 30lb 12oz.

After years of trying to get another twenty-pound fish I had broken my personal best on my first serious day's piking on the Stour. I sacked the fish and called out to a friend to witness it. When he had arrived some fifteen minutes later I removed the fish from the sack, took some photos and carefully returned it to the water. We both watched it swim back out toward the main current where it disappeared from view. With two hours left that day I continued roach fishing, taking a fish of 2lb 13oz – again a personal best. The following day I took my first three-pound roach at 3lb 1oz. Now this is the sort of fishing that dreams are made of.

For the rest of this season pike were very much at the top of my list. This was to be my best season for pike, and it seemed that nearly every weekend I went pike fishing at least one twenty came my way. Towards the end of the season I ventured on to the Royalty for the odd day, and this was to be the scene of one of the best day's piking I have ever had.

It was, I think, my tenth visit to the Royalty. My intended target area was a swim where I had seen a good fish take the bait the previous week, only then to drop it before I had chance to set the hooks. I never actually got there. Passing by a slack from which I had taken an obliging 11lb fish twice before, I decided to see if it was still there. My

The 30lb mark is broken at last by 12oz.

bait had hardly been in the water a minute when the float shot under the surface. This fish turned out not to be the expected eleven but a fish of over 20lb. In a short space of time three more good fish came to the net. I honestly cannot remember what the order was, but the weights were: 14lb 7oz, 22lb 6oz, 24lb 3oz, and 27lb 8oz. As I was playing the third twenty it shook the bait fish from its mouth at the surface on its way to the net. The bait fish was taken almost immediately by another pike that I estimated to be over 20lb, but which unfortunately I did not catch. I took a few group shots of the three 20lb fish and returned them to the water.

Every year the Royalty produces at least one fish over the magic 30lb mark. It must rate as one of the premier pike stretches of the Hampshire Avon, but although the pike are there, they do not often come out. I spend a few days each year in search of pike on this venue and have taken only four fish over 20lb. The fourth was a 26lb fish taken in the same season and from the same swim as the other three 20lb fish. It may well have been the same fish that was there on the aforementioned occasion. Often a large fish will be captured only once on this stretch of water. The reasons for this are twofold.

The first reason is the abundance of food fish. Not only are coarse fish (including lots of bream) available, but the Avon below the main road bridge also has a large head of sea species, combined with the annual run of both sea trout and salmon. With this quantity of prey fish available, the pike are bound to reach a much higher than average weight than anywhere else on the river. In my opinion, and I must state that this is only theoretical, a lot of the pike caught from the Royalty itself may not be resident fish. With Christchurch Harbour only a short distance downstream, most of the pike may be resident in the harbour area, or in the vicinity of the Clay Pool where the Rivers Avon and Stour meet. All other freshwater species are there, so why not the pike? You may think that some of these must surely be caught, but the fact is that the rules governing methods of fishing in this area are restrictive and the amount of water vast. This has meant that no one to my knowledge has in fact given these areas of the river a decent amount of time. I for one have never even tried fishing there for any species. Any pike that wish to live their lives in this area, only needing to move to shallower areas in time of spawning, will therefore have a reasonably good chance of avoiding capture.

The second and worst reason is that the ruling on the Royalty is that pike should not be returned to the water – this is stated on the day tickets – although the rule is not enforced. While it remains stamped

The three twenties from the Royalty.

on the ticket, however, it allows inconsiderate anglers the opportunity to kill pike! I say inconsiderate as anyone doing so deprives other anglers of the chance of catching what may well be the best pike they are ever likely to see. In the case of a large 30lb fish being killed, it may also jeopardize the possibility of the Hampshire Avon once again producing a record fish.

Summer Piking

Well, that has dealt with winter piking, but what about summer fishing? For me, pike fishing does not start until October at the earliest these days. This is firstly for reasons of conservation, and secondly because pike are rather thin in the summer when compared with their normal winter condition. However, I have been known to cast the odd plug around in the summer months. The first fish over 20lb that I took on a plug was the direct result of the fact that I used something that up until that time I had regarded as a joke.

113

I was plug fishing on the middle Stour when Richard Graham arrived on the opposite bank and engaged in a bit of fish spotting. When he got level with me, he asked me the usual questions and I replied that only small pike seemed to be about. I literally asked if he fancied a laugh, and switched over to a red and white Heddon Crazy Crawler. For anyone who is not familiar with this plug but who has a good imagination, its antics are similar to a demented fat frog with its legs out of synchronization. I cast the plug out and retrieved it slowly to much raucous laughter. I cast out for a second time, stating that it caught pike but only small ones. The words were hardly out of my mouth when a pike whacked it from the surface. I had no idea of the size of this fish as by then both of us were laughing so much that neither of us had seen the pike actually take the lure. I leaned into it and suddenly realized that this was not a small fish – this was probably due to the fact that it took off 3ft into the air from less than 2ft of water. All our laughing stopped and Richard made the obvious statement that it looked like a good fish!

Once I had the fish on the bank I got the forceps out to remove the hooks. Taking the fish from the folds of the landing net I realized that the plug was well inside its mouth. In fact, it was at the entrance to the throat cavity. Whatever the pike had thought the plug was I do not know, but one thing is for certain: it definitely wanted to eat it. This fish weighed 20lb 2oz. With the plug no longer regarded as a joke, it saw a lot of use and accounted for another fish at 20lb 4oz two days later, plus lots of doubles over a period of time. The plug is now beaten around so much that the action no longer works. As a summer plug it was without doubt the best pike plug I had ever used, both in providing entertainment and getting fish on the bank! These days, however, plug fishing is very much an occasional affair for me.

Deadbait or livebait fishing in the summer catches an awful lot of big pike. Having lost much of their weight during their spawning activities, pike feed far more voraciously in the summer months to regain their condition. The fact that they have not seen an angler's bait for three months means that their usual caution when taking dead or live fish is non-existent. Whilst this means that the success rate in catching large pike during this period will be high, certain considerations should be taken into account. Summer pike put up a spectacular fight and have no respect for weed-beds! The chances of losing a fish because it has gone right through a dense bed of weed and keeps on going are extremely high. Should you win this battle, other problems can occur. Once on the bank, pike are prone to gassing up due to an extensive fight combined with low oxygen levels. In such a situation it is very likely that a good fish may suffer badly enough to cause its death.

On a water that receives more than its fair share of pressure, the same pike may be caught a number of times in a very short period. Eventually someone is bound to get it wrong either by losing the fish in a weed-bed complete with trebles, or by hooking the fish deep enough to cause extensive damage. The latter particularly holds true when fishing deadbaits as pike in the summer move even less when taking such a bait. Bearing this in mind, it is up to the individual's ethics as to whether he or she is prepared to take the risks involved in summer pike fishing! Although I do catch a fair amount of pike during the summer, these are fish that have been taken accidentally while fishing for eels. I have seen a number of large pike taken in the first weeks of the season, and the temptation for some to fish for pike is high when other species are not being co-operative.

One such occasion on 21 June in the 1991–2 season started with the capture of a large pike, Mark 'Big Nose' Hately having given up on the tench to try his hand at pike fishing. At 1.50 p.m. I saw Big Nose gesticulating to me that he had caught a large pike. Collecting my camera gear, scales and weigh sling, I went across to do the honours. As the sack was removed from the water it became apparent that it was indeed a good fish – at 44in in length and with a girth of 20in, the fish weighed an impressive 29lb 3oz. After the photos were taken and fish returned, a certain amount of rebuke from me included such comments as 'Shame it wasn't caught in the winter when it would have been thirty plus.' Mark was unimpressed by this and continued to fish for pike.

He landed a number of fish over the next few days, including another high 20lb one. Two of the fish he hooked caused immense enjoyment for the other nearby anglers who were fishing for tench and carp. The first was caught while he was fishing a swim known as Bonanza Point on the other side of the lake. He hooked into a double-figure pike that seemed to think it was a member of the flying-fish family – it spent far more time out of the water than it did in. The fish was eventually landed and Mark proceeded to lift it up in the landing net to show us, whereupon it went crazy and slashed the net to pieces. Fortunately, it was still over the water at the time and it soon made off towards the middle of the lake. The following few minutes caused much amusement as he struggled to get rod and reel through the remains of his net. The pike was then landed again, this time without any further drama.

Later in the same day the inevitable happened. Still fishing from Bonanza Point, Mark hit a fish only two rod lengths out that he could not control. The fish finally stopped running when it was nearly into my swim some 60yd from where it had originally started. No amount of pulling would get the fish to move and it had gone through some 30yd of dense weed by then. After fifteen minutes or so Mark came round to declare that it was a big fish as he had seen it when it took off. Pulling for a break was out of the question, and he announced that he intended to go in after it. After a bankside conference, it was decided that this was the best course of action – providing that one of the lifebelts was taken out as a precaution.

Mark made his way back round the lake, collected a lifebelt and proceeded to swim out to where the pike was, pulling the line from the weed on the way. Not one of us had given consideration to the resident cob swan which hated everything that moved! As Mark approached the half-way mark, the swan appeared from the other side of the island and spotted Mark immediately. It was not amused. The swan assumed an aggressive attitude and covered the distance in about thirty seconds flat. Fortunately for him the swan did not complete its attack and merely circled as Mark frantically waved his arms to fend it away. Remarks were made by Mark to the effect that those assembled on the bank should offer assistance! To be honest, not one of us would have been capable anyway as we were rolling around in fits of laughter. Eventually, the swan left him and he got to the end of the line, retrieving the snap tackle from the weeds minus any sign of the pike.

Realizing the folly of summer pike fishing, Mark decided that the interests of the pike were more important and decided to leave them alone until the weed had died down later in the year. News of the large pike he had captured had got round by now, and suddenly everyone wanted to go pike fishing. The largest of the pike was caught three more times to my knowledge over the next two weeks. A number of fish were lost in the weed, and it stands to reason that some of these were probably deep hooked and may well have died as a result. One large fish was found in distress some weeks after the season opened, and after subsequently catching the fish with the aid of landing net, the concerned angler found the pike to have two size 6 trebles lodged in its throat. Fortunately, the hooks were removed and the fish survived. This was one very lucky pike. It was caught the same winter by the angler that saved its life and now appears to be in perfect health. This incident had resulted in the controlling club imposing a ban on pike fishing until October. The ban has caused mixed feelings, but I for one am in total agreement with the club on this issue! Pike these days have a hard enough time as it is, so let's put them first and leave them well alone until winter.

7

Roach

Fishing for roach is easy; these delightful fish can be most accommodating. Their distribution is widespread throughout the UK – they are found in most lakes and reservoirs, and in the majority of river systems. At times, the fish will take the bait almost as soon as you have cast in and often before the float has had a chance to settle. So, we have established that roach fishing is easy, and if a bag of roach is all that you want then you will have a successful day's fishing on most outings. If, on the other hand, it is big roach that you are after – in other words, over 2lb – then the approach and, in some respects, personal discipline can prove somewhat different.

It is entirely possible to go to your local lake or river and fish through shoals of roach, eventually breaking through the magic 2lb barrier. However, a preferable approach is to go to a lake or section of a river where there are no outstandingly large shoals of roach, knowing that if you do contact a lone roach then the chances are it is going to be over 2lb.

My approach to roach fishing is very much along the lines of the latter, and it certainly does work. My best river fish of 3lb 5oz came from a stretch of the Hampshire Avon that holds very few roach. There are one or two swims along the stretch that hold a certain amount of smaller roach, but for the main it is a very understocked fishery. It was the first large roach I had from this fishery in three seasons – that is where the discipline comes in. There is one other advantage in adopting this sort of approach, as if the chosen stretch is so hard you can guarantee that there will always be a vacant swim. Often the venue will be empty on the day you choose to fish, giving you the opportunity to search the length of the stretch systematically. I am not saying that if you were to camp out on such a water for a week or so you would catch a monster roach – I have already tried that approach and it didn't work! What I am saying, however, is that if you keep going back to a water that fits this description, eventually the chances are that a big fish may well come your way.

The problems that are involved with fishing this sort of venue are many. One such problem is that the fish will not see an awful lot of bait and therefore will be feeding almost exclusively on natural foods.

A 2lb 7oz roach caught the day my daughter, Janine, was born.

Fortunately, roach are inquisitive creatures and seem to investigate anything that is white, so if they are feeding then they can usually be persuaded to take bread or maggots. Of the two, maggot is likely to be the favourite bait. As well as the more frequently used white maggot, I have also had success with red maggot when fishing for roach and always include a few in amongst the whites as a change bait.

This seems as good a place as any to recount the events that led up to the capture of my best river roach from this type of water.

A Personal Best River Roach

The capture of this roach started out with my decision to change the species I was pursuing while I was fishing the Hampshire Avon. I had originally decided on a day's pike fishing, and on arrival on the Hampshire Avon I started catching a few dace for bait. After an hour or so I had taken a number of dace plus two roach of around ½lb. As the roach were obviously feeding and the river was carrying some extra colour, I decided to shelve the pike fishing and go for roach instead.

Only having maggots, I managed to obtain half a loaf of bread from Ron Smith and then went upstream. On the third trot down I hooked a good fish that, after a short fight, turned out to be a 2lb 11oz roach. Ron jokingly said that he deserved half the fish's weight as it was his bread! I had to disagree, but it was nice of him to give me the bread, and he duly took some photos of the fish. Two hours passed and as I had not taken another fish I moved downstream. After another couple of hours' hard fishing I had got another four fish up to a pound or so to show for my efforts.

With my roach head then firmly on, all thoughts of pike fishing over the next few days were forgotten. The next day I set out for roach again and took five fish, the best being 2lb 3oz and once again on the bread. By the day after, all the colour had gone from the river and I switched over to maggots. After two hours of hard trotting without a bite, the float finally slipped away and I was rewarded with another roach. This one turned out to be 2lb 6oz. The rest of the day was uneventful apart from a solitary dace of around 4oz.

My fourth day saw a lot more anglers on this venue as word had got around by now, and, of course, it was Sunday. I spent the morning wandering between different stretches, and ended up on a hard roach stretch with only one other angler present. I was in two minds as to what to fish for, but decided to go for barbel. I spent the first hour baiting a few swims up with hemp and corn in the hope that I would find some barbel. As none showed I decided to have another go for the roach, walking up to a swim in which I had seen the odd fish before, but which I had never fished. The river was still up and rather more pacey than is normal on this stretch. The reason for this was that a large tree trunk had gone through one of the hatches on the lower weir, thereby allowing water to escape at a much faster rate.

I chucked in a dozen maggots and set the float at 5ft, the swim being around 6ft deep. With the first trot down the swim about 5–6yd away, the float slipped under the surface. The strike met with a solid thump and I was in. The fight was over within a couple of minutes and an immaculate roach weighing well over 3lb appeared on the surface. With nerves of steel, I slid it calmly across the net . . . well, to be honest, I was in a right state! At these times you expect everything to go wrong, so I was relieved to get it into the net and on to the bank without the size 14 hook pulling out. Just then the bailiff showed up in time to witness and weigh the fish, which looked in perfect condition. The needle registered just under 3lb 5oz, although it would perhaps have been heavier later in the season. The roach measured 16in long and had a girth of 14¼in. With the vital statistics and photographs taken, the fish was sacked just in case I could manage another brace – but this was not to be.

After another three hours without a bite I moved swims. The first cast saw a 2lb 2oz roach grace the net, and then nothing for the rest of the day. I could not be bothered to photograph the two-pounder and slipped it straight back. It is terrible putting back an immaculate roach without taking photos, and if I had caught it first or in the same swim as the three-pounder then no doubt I would have done.

The only thing left to do then was to get the scales verified on the way home. Upon checking with John Level, the scales proved to be ½oz on the light side thereby making the fish slightly over 3lb 5oz. But who's splitting hairs? A new personal best!

Another problem, if it can be called that, with fishing for roach at understocked venues is that often they will be seen rolling in the last light of the day but will totally ignore your bait. This does nothing to inspire confidence in the bait you are using or in your personal ability as an angler – at these times you feel that you should have caught, and there is no answer as to why you did not. Still, if all the answers were obvious then would we still be fishing? Having just said that there is no answer to this, I have realized that there may be an explanation to these impossible rolling fish.

Most anglers are under the impression that when fish are rolling on the surface they are doing so as a prelude to feeding. Instead, consider this. Roach, or indeed any other species, do not need to roll on the surface when they are about to feed – they are more likely to be actually feeding. The time of day that most fish are seen rolling on or near the surface is during the early part of the morning or as the hours of darkness approach. These times happen to coincide with the emergence of most of our native water insects. Having spent the greater part of their lives living in the water, these insects now have to make their way to the surface to emerge from their aquatic environment. They then have to dry themselves out before finally taking off as adult flying insects to breed. At the stage in their lives between leaving the lake or river bottom and flying off, they are at their most vulnerable, as they are likely to gain the attention of fish.

I therefore think that it is fairly safe to assume that most of the fish we see rolling are actually preoccupied with feeding on these emerging nymphs. If this is the case, then the chances of such a roach taking a bait which is fished on or near the bottom are going to be remote. If, on the other hand, the maggots are fished on a float rod within 2ft of the surface, the chances are that a roach may well be persuaded to take a bait. There may even be a case for the fly rod being brought into action should this approach fail. Now, all this talk of flies and nymphs most definitely falls into the category of an armchair theory. Although I have caught a number of roach during the closed season when trout fishing using nymph, I have never considered trying for them when they are rolling during the season. I can assure you that I will put this theory into practice when I next have large roach taking the mickey out of me!

Getting away from theory, there are two standard methods of fishing for roach: one is to float fish for them and the other is to ledger. When float fishing I will only use a centre pin as this gives greater control of the tackle, allowing me to hold the float back, if needed, for the whole length of the swim. Although this can be achieved with a fixed-spool reel to some extent, it is not as smooth in its presentation as a centre pin. The pin also allows you to overshoot the float by at least a BB without the problem of it going under every time you pay out line – as occurs when using a fixed spool. Also, with a pin you are in direct contact with the float at all times – this means that you will miss less bites and, at times, will feel the fish take the bait before the float has even gone down.

A 2lb 10oz fish caught in the summer.

When summer roach fishing, one of the best methods is to use hemp in conjunction with the float. The ideal summer roach swim for fishing the stick float and hemp consists of a steady glide at around 4ft deep or more. Roach can be spotted in these depths on both the Avon and Stour, and time must be spent walking the banks to find the fish before actual fishing commences. Armed with a bucket of hemp, each likely looking swim should be baited with a couple of dozen grains in such a way that you will be able to watch them as they drift down with the current. Keep a steady stream of hemp going in for around fifteen minutes or so in each chosen swim. If the roach do not show themselves in this time, move on and repeat the exercise until roach are located. Once found, fish for them using as light a float as possible. The shot should be arranged shirt-button style, with small shot such as No. 8 used. These must be placed on the line in pairs as this will help to avoid many false bites. Alternatively, styl-type weights can be used.

Hookbait can consist of a single tare or a grain of hemp, or you can use the black plastic bead method by gluing one direct to the shank.

The bead needs to be slightly bigger than a single grain of hemp. When using the latter approach it is useful to carry a bottle of typist's correction fluid – this is used to paint the upper part of the hook and knot white so that the bead more accurately simulates the hemp seed. The advantage of using the bead method is twofold: first, it saves fiddling around with hemp on the hook; and second, the roach seem to hang on to plastic longer than hemp, thereby giving you a far greater chance of hitting bites.

Now, to the actual fishing. If you intend to use hemp on its own then the best 'hookbait' is the plastic bead. This will catch the roach and most definitely is not another armchair theory. The method is simple. Set the float so that the hook is kept 1ft off the bottom. Throw in a dozen or so grains of hemp, and cast the float in amongst the free offerings with as little disturbance as possible. The bites will mostly be indicated by either the usual dragging under or by the fact that the float will not settle correctly. If the float does not cock in the usual manner, this will indicate that fish are taking the bait on the drop. The amount of time it takes to cock after casting in can soon be gauged; any delay and a strike should be made.

The roach may move right up near the surface once they get a taste for the hemp and will often be seen boiling within the first couple of feet. Should this occur, catching them becomes almost impossible. There are two methods for getting them back lower in the water.

The method most often written about is to stop the feed going in. This will of course work, as because the roach no longer get the dozen or so bits of hemp, they will soon move back lower in the water. The problem with this method is that they are also likely to move back downstream and go off the feed for a while, and as soon as you start to reintroduce the feed, you will more or less be starting all over again. The other method, and the one I use, is to up the rate of feed dramatically, throwing in a good handful for two or three casts. This will get the fish to follow the hemp downstream as it falls to the bottom. They will therefore be pushed back to the bed of the river at a spot lower down the swim. They will then actually start to feed on the hemp that has settled there. You can then cut the feed back to the original dozen grains per cast, and the roach will soon be back feeding as before. Once they have eaten all the offerings on the bottom and have moved back to the loose feed, they may gradually move up in the water again. Should this happen, adopt the same procedure once again.

When using tare as hookbait, two or three seeds every third cast or so will be needed to supplement the hemp as loose feed. Unlike with

A brace of Avon roach: 3lb 3oz and 3lb.

hemp, there is little advantage in using plastic instead of tare on the hook, as the tares are simple to hook and stay on well. Roach will search out the tare in amongst the free offerings and bites will be much the same as with straight hemp fishing. The problems of fish moving up in the water are somewhat reduced when fishing hemp and tare. If this is the case, then you may ask, why bother with straight hemp in the first place? The reason for this is the fact that hemp is not a particularly filling feed – it takes an awful lot of hemp to overfeed a fair-sized shoal of roach. On the other hand, tares are very filling and it does not take long to feed them off. Hemp literally goes straight through fish. Anyone who has used hemp will know that often hemp will be coming from the vent of the fish as the photos are taken. And just have a look in the bottom of the sack after the fish have been returned – yet more hemp! On the other hand, if you try to find a tare in the sack or any other hookbait you are using you will have a hard job.

Hemp and tare fishing is not the only method for catching roach on the float rod, it just happens to be one of the best for hot summer days. Another method is to use hemp and caster. This works exceptionally well and is not too cost-prohibitive as 2 pints of caster to 6 pints or more of hemp should be ample to cover a number of swims in a day. My best day's roach fishing in terms of numbers of quality fish from one swim came on a day when the temperature was well into the eighties and when I used the hemp and tare method.

An Excellent Day's Roaching

I had moved from Blandford up river to Sturminster Newton in the winter. With my new house being less than a mile from the river, it did not take me long to get around to having a look at what was on offer as far as spotting was concerned. The next summer, I found a nice-looking straight with a slow, even pace and with trees lining one bank. I was just about to climb one of the trees when I noticed a couple of roach just out from the bank. I moved cautiously between the trees and spotted some more. The river bed near the tree-lined bank had quite a few cabbages growing along it, but to what extent I could not see. In the next hour or so I observed that a large shoal of roach were living in this swim. The roach rarely moved out of the cabbages themselves, so fishing for them in amongst the vegetation would have proved impossible. My first thought was to cut a swim in the cabbages themselves. After some consideration, however, I threw this idea out; after all, by doing so I would probably destroy the reason they were there in the first place. I decided eventually to climb a tree to get a better view of the swim. The bottom was clearly visible to about a third of the way across and consisted of 5ft of water over clean gravel. As it slopped back up to the other side, I could see a few cabbages in the next third of the river bed. I could also see a few roach moving amongst these cabbages, although there were not as many fish on this side. The clear channel through the middle was the obvious place to catch the fish if I could convince them to feed there, and so I formulated a plan to this end.

I went back home and collected some hemp, and then climbed back up the tree with bucket in hand to watch for results. I started to introduce a few offerings into the swim but got little response. I then upped the feed rate, but still there was no response. Thwarted in my quest, I decided to put plan B into operation the following day. I liquidized around half a gallon of cooked hemp and threw this into the head of the swim. The result was a milky cloud which made its way slowly downstream. A lot of this went into the cabbages and for a while I could not see a thing. Once the cloud had cleared sufficiently, I could see that the roach had begun to move around the swim and so I started to throw some loose feed in. The roach intercepted quite a lot of this and I fed another two pints quickly into the swim. I continued this baiting over the next few days, adding a few tares to the hemp. All the baiting up was done in the middle of the day, and soon the roach were out of the cabbages as soon as I put the bait into the swim.

On the day that I decided to fish the swim, I went to the other side and introduced the liquidized hemp straight into the middle of the river just up from the swim. I moved down to a point right opposite where I had been spotting, and threw in a few loose offerings followed closely by my tackle which I had baited with a single tare. The first trot down saw a sail-away bite which resulted in a roach of over 2lb coming to the net. Within the next hour more roach followed, including another two over this mark.

On the day concerned I did not have any film in my camera, but not wanting to be without photographs I telephoned *Angler's Mail* to report what I had caught, asking them if they would like to send a reporter down to record the catch on film. They agreed and I furnished them with details of the venue. With a photographer on the way, I went back to my fishing. By the time the photographer arrived an hour and a half later I had taken a few more fish, including another three roach over 2lb, one of which was my personal best at 2lb 12oz.

On arrival, the photographer took the relevant details of line strength and methods, then each fish was witnessed and weighed in turn. Photos were taken and the fish were placed into the keep net, and once the loose ends had been tied up the photographer went his way. I decided that I had had enough for the day and returned the fish I had caught. It was then that I realized that the keep net just was not suitable for retaining quality fish – when I lifted the net out there were a number of scales in the bottom that had been lost by the fish. Upon further examination, most of the roach had lost a few scales and looked in a bit of a sorry state. These fish had not had a scale out of place when they went into the net so there was no doubt that the damage had been caused by my ignorance.

The details of my catch appeared on a whole page in *Angler's Mail* the following week and then the week after that I was informed by a committee member of the local angling club that I was going to be banned from the club for using an illegal bait. The accusation was actually incorrect as I had been fishing in a stretch of water that was not controlled by the club. I did not bother to dispute this, however, as I had already bought a house in Salisbury and was due to move in four weeks' time. When the committee had their meeting I did not attend and subsequently I was banned. The controlling club concerned now has no such ban and I have been informed that I am able to join again if I so wish. The price of fame does have its drawbacks!

Sadly, this stretch of the upper Stour has suffered from a very high fish loss in recent years due to farm pollution and a lot of the large shoals of fish are no longer there. One angler I know who lives within a mile of the water no longer fishes for roach in this area now, even though it was not long ago that he fished nowhere else. It is a sad fact of life that a once-productive river can be virtually or entirely wiped out overnight!

On stretches of the Stour in particular, and mostly around the middle to upper reaches, there are a number of elderberry trees. The elderberries themselves are very much a seasonal bait when they become ripe toward the end of the summer and into autumn. At the point of ripening, some of these naturally will drop into the water and fish soon become accustomed to taking the juicy morsels with abandon. It is simplicity itself to fish and introduce bait with elderberries.

There are two methods by which elderberries can be introduced into a swim. The first involves picking lots of bunches and throwing them in by hand, but this is a rather messy business. Alternatively, you can use the method I employ. Set up a pike rod with 15lb line and attach a 2oz lead, and then cast it into one of the overhanging elderberry trees. All you need to do now is shake the tree with the aid of the pike rod so that the ripe berries are introduced into the swim. Roach will not worry unduly, providing that you do not create too much disturbance when you do this. All you have to do now is to follow up with a stick float and elderberry in the same manner as you would hemp or tares. Personally, I do not introduce any other bait into the water when fishing this method. I do know that some anglers advocate the use of hemp when using elderberries, but quite honestly I cannot see any point in this as it is defeating the object somewhat. As long as the berries are on the trees they will work as an excellent bait – that is providing that the river is reasonably clear.

Some success can be obtained at times when elderberries are not evident, but as this is rather limited I see little point in trying to save some for future use. Also, if the river is heavily coloured then they are of no use whatsoever and baits such as bread will be far more productive. Fish spotting can still be of use when intending to use elderberries, as by climbing a few of the trees and shaking them roach will show themselves in much the same manner as described earlier. If none show within the first hour of fishing then the chances are that they are not there and you may as well move down to the next tree. The reason for this is simple: if the swim that you have chosen has far less ripe fruits than the next one, the roach will be at the latter as the pickings will be far better. By this simple fact, you can be sure that one of the swims will have more roach in it than any other!

In clear water conditions another method that works extremely well is stalking. Now for most, stalking means walking along the banks until a good roach is spotted and then fishing for it. Me? I cheat. If I spot a good roach I don't actually fish for it immediately.

Before describing what I do, I should first point out that the hemp and tare/caster method is of little use with this approach. This is the time for hemp in conjunction with something that can be seen. It is always worthwhile to include a few tares in amongst the free offerings for reasons that will become apparent later. The most obvious baits are sweetcorn, or maggot if the visibility is exceptionally good. On one river I fish, corn is a total waste of time and maggot is the only bait worth using. The main reason for this is that very few people fish this river and the roach have no idea what corn is. I myself fish it so infrequently that I cannot be bothered trying to educate them! This river will be dealt with separately further on.

Anyway, on to the method. Once I have seen a fish I bait slightly upstream of where I spotted it, choosing a swim that has a clean, fine, gravel bottom and preferably some sort of cover – for example, weed or an overhanging bush. I then introduce a good handful of hemp laced with corn and move on to find more fish. (I only tend to use maggot when spotting and stalking in the winter, so I will deal with this later.) Once I have covered the length of the water that I intend to fish and have baited a few swims that I feel the roach will move into, I start to fish. Unless I have seen an exceptional fish I always start at one end of the fishery and cover the swims systematically. The main advantage when using this method is that I know exactly which swims should have fish in them. There is no need for me to creep along the bank to find my quarry, and I only have to exercise caution as I approach each swim.

I use a soft-action quivertip rod for stalking roach. The quivertip is of no use during the actual stalking, but it saves me carrying an extra rod should I decide to continue fishing into the dark, or if conditions change and I can no longer see into the water. The line strength to use is 4lb, along with a simple link ledger consisting of a swivel to which a short length of line is tied. This enables me to add or subtract swan shot as flow dictates. The hook length is around 18in, usually 4lb Kryston with a size 10 hook on the end.

As I creep up to each swim I look in to see if any roach are present. Once I have spotted one, I lower a single grain of corn gently into the

A 2lb 11oz roach taken whilst stalking.

swim and position it so that I can see it clearly. I will then watch the corn until such time as the fish I want picks it up. A hard, controlled strike should then make contact with the fish – using the soft-action rod means that I can strike that much harder and quicker without the worry of pulling out of the fish or causing a breakage. Once landed, I weigh and sack the fish and then check the swim again for any other large roach. If any other fish are present I continue in the same manner, and once the swim shows that no more large roach are in evidence, I photograph and return any I have caught. I then check the rest of the baited swims in rotation until I run out of daylight. Then, should I decide to continue fishing, it is on to the quivertip rod – this is the reason for the tares remaining in the feed.

It can safely be assumed that not all the fish I see in a day's fishing will be caught during the hours of daylight. Some will see me as I set about stalking them and refuse to feed; others may become spooked as I hook another fish and prove equally difficult to catch. Having decided to stay on for an hour or so after dark there is no place for sweetcorn on the hook, unless you do not mind the attention of the 'river curse'! Personally, I do not mind catching large eels one bit, but the problem in the Wessex rivers is that the eels are not generally large and they simply adore sweetcorn! If you are brave enough to attempt to catch roach after dark on corn, then sooner rather than later you will be plagued with one eel after another. Once they are in the swim you do not have a hope of them leaving you in peace and the answer here is to fish tare.

Eels will take tare on the odd occasion but only one or two passing eels should give you any problems. If eels come through the swim they will soon eat any corn that is left from the day's baiting and then move on to the next area. The last thing you want at night is for an eel to take the bait. First, they will cut the odds of you taking any roach right down as they wriggle around on the end of the line, alerting the roach to the fact that someone is still fishing. Second, they make a real mess of end tackle, and you will spend more time tying hooks and swivels back on than actually fishing – see if you can stand remaking the tackle every few minutes!

The standard approach for ledgering at night is to use a rod with an isotope fixed to the end. There are various ways of fixing this to the end of the rod, but the method I use is to glue it into place using a clear epoxy resin. Any method that suits is fine, so long as the line does not catch. You also need a low chair in which to make yourself comfortable and a rod rest; bites at night are usually slow and deliberate affairs. The simple link ledger can still be used, although a fixed lead attached to a Drennan ring with a 4in length of line will produce far better results. I keep the weight down to a ½oz or so and increase the length of tail to around 2ft – this is also attached to the Drennan ring.

The hook length needs to be slightly lighter than the main line so that if a fish is lost due to breakage it will not have to drag the lead around. Hooks should be extremely sharp and in size 12 or 10 if you use two tares – Drennan specialist hooks are ideal for this method of fishing. Hold the rod at all times, using the rest to steady the quivertip. I do not strike at every pull but wait for a definite indication. Fast, sharp pulls are often likely to be the result of line bites as fish moving through the swim touch the line and move off quickly. Any strike that is made on these indications will cut down my chances of a decent fish and make foul hooking a distinct possibility. Most times roach will take the bait in such a manner as to leave you in no doubt as to when they are hooked. Contrary to popular belief, big roach hang themselves when you are ledgering! I will now go on to deal with the river that I used to fish with maggot only.

Fishing the River Allen

The River Allen rises above the village of Monktown just short of the main Blandford–Salisbury road and was once a glorious river. In its upper reaches it is very much a winter bourn. It rarely, if ever, flows from its highest point of origin and its main spring is situated between this point and Wimborne St Giles. This main spring lies ten miles above Wimborne Minster where, just below the town centre, the Allen flows into the river – in fact, it is one of the main tributaries of the Stour.

The Allen is classed as a pure chalk-stream for its entire length. When it reaches Wimborne St Giles, part of the river is diverted to feed an artificial, privately owned lake. Once it makes its way down to Standbridge it then becomes victim to a borehole which abstracts up to 5 million gallons of water a day. For a river that at times only has a daily flow equalling this, it could be deemed an excessively high abstraction! Fortunately, however, at this point it is fed by the Gussage Brook. Once the river has travelled a further two miles it reaches Witchampton Mill, and at this point the hatches controlling the flow

A 2lb 15oz fish caught from the River Allen. Notice how this fish tapers quickly towards the tail. If it had not been so badly proportioned, it would have weighed well over 3lb.

131

are high. Above these hatches the river is of little interest to the coarse angler, which is just as well as the river is preserved solely for fly fishing – in actual fact, this is the case for most of its length.

The reason I have mapped out the river to this point is that there has been little pollution above it. However, below the mill, which until recently has produced paper, pollution does occur all too frequently – for example, during the Christmas period in 1983 there was a very bad case of pollution below the mill which resulted in an extensive fish kill; salmon, trout, large grayling and roach being amongst the casualties. The River Allen at one time held the record for grayling, so this was a catastrophe as far as coarse anglers were concerned. Although the trout fishermen on the stretch were also affected to an extent, as most of their fish come from stocking before the start of the season the loss for them was not as great. Having received such a major setback, the river became virtually ignored by coarse fishermen except such stalwarts as the late Owen Wentworth. Although the majority of the resident stocks had perished, a few had somehow survived and these became very large as the available food now had to feed far fewer mouths.

In 1987 I joined a club that has the fishing rights to a section of the river just above the town of Wimborne. Owen Wentworth had often mentioned to me that there were large roach to be caught from this river if I was able to find them. For its entire length, the stretch is highly visible at most times of the year and my first visit to the river consisted of a fish-spotting exercise. I located a few roach, none of which were above 1lb, but also a small head of grayling plus lots of brown trout averaging 1lb or so.

When I first started to fish for the grayling I found that some good roach started to appear in the odd swim after a few maggots had been introduced. Having now seen the roach potential, I decided that hemp and corn would be the way to catch them. I failed miserably. The only fish that showed any interest were the trout, grayling, eels and another species that I had not seen up until then – chub, which although not large, averaged 2–3lb.

The only thing that got the roach interested was maggot. Now with the average depth of this chalk-stream being about 2ft and the size of the river small, float fishing was totally out of the question. The only viable method was bottom fishing. I decided to find out first just how many good roach the river held, and to this end arrived with 2 gallons of maggots to bait all the likely swims on the stretch.

The whole day was designated to finding roach rather than actually fishing for them, and the amount of roach I found on this day was quite incredible. I found odd fish throughout the length of the water and discovered two main shoals in two totally different swims. The first was at a bend in the river where the depth was about 5ft. It dropped from 2ft into this hole and was surrounded on all sides by weed-beds. Fifteen roach in the swim topped 2lb, one of which was an easy three-pounder. The second swim was located on a 30yd straight between two sharp bends and had an average depth of only 2ft. Bushes and small trees covered half the actual width of the river on the far side at this point, and the roach were resident under the cover they afforded. This shoal had nine fish that would top 2lb and two fish that I thought would be over 3lb. These two swims received a lot of attention over the next two seasons!

The approach that I used actually to fish the river was to bait the two main swims with maggot, using a dropper in the deeper swim and loose feeding into a gap between the trees on the other. I then left the swims and spent some time wandering around trying to pick off the odd roach from elsewhere. Periodically, my path crossed the baited swims.

Once fish have been spotted the stalking can begin. Waiting for the fish to go out of the swim before casting in is a must, and when they have done so the bait can be positioned in such a way that it can be seen. With maggot being so small, this can only be accomplished on days when conditions are perfect – in other words, when it is bright and there is no wind at all. The river also has to be gin-clear. As the Allen is a chalk-stream the water was clear for most of the time, but the days when all the other conditions needed for success were present were few and far between. If the conditions were not favourable but fish could still be spotted, then I used to rely on the quivertip and fixed paternoster.

In the swim where the water was deeper, fish could be taken by fishing maggot on the drop. By using the minimum of shot on the line 2ft above the hook, picking out a double maggot from a few loose-fed baits was relatively simple. The bait should be watched on its descent, with striking taking place as a roach takes the bait – John Medlow caught his personal best roach of 2lb 12oz using this method from the tail-end of the deep swim.

The best fish that I hooked on the Allen was the large fish in the deep swim. After two seasons of picking the days on which to attempt to catch this fish, I finally managed to hook it. I had taken a few fish on previous visits to the swim, including on two occasions a brace of 2lb roach. All was going well when a large pike that must have been approaching 20lb appeared from under the bank and hit my hooked roach before I had a chance to do anything about it. Now I like pike, but on this occasion I cursed this fish no end. It had cost me my personal best roach and I was not pleased! The fact is though that it is very unlikely that the pike would have attacked a roach of this size under normal circumstances. The reason that it took the fish in this case was that the roach was showing signs of distress and was acting in such a way as to trigger the pike's natural instincts to take a sick or injured fish. This is the basic reason a pike exists – in other words, to thin out the sick or injured. Knowing this, I had to accept that as a direct result of hooking the roach I had caused its death.

When John hooked his personal best roach the following season the pike was still in residence. Knowing about the experience that I had with this pike, John had an advantage. It was 16 June when Andy Harman and I accompanied John to the same water. We all watched as the roach took the bait and John finally hooked it (this was after it had twice picked up the bait whilst being masked from John's eye by other roach). As he was playing the fish the pike appeared from under

This 2lb 12oz roach was actually hit by a big pike on the way in and lost just a few scales before it was swept from the water.

the bank and we all saw it at more or less the same instant. As the pike surged forward, John leaned into the fish to pull it out of the way. Luckily, the pike missed it – just! It was so close to taking the roach that it actually dislodged some scales from the roach as it passed. These could be seen flickering in the bright sunlight as they made their way to the bottom. Before it had time to turn around for another go, I had the landing net under the fish and it was out. The pike moved back under the bank and we got on with the job of weighing and photographing the roach. Needless to say, the remaining roach had all dispersed. Later in the day, Andy caught one of the loners some distance further upstream by stalking. This was his then personal best at 2lb 6oz. I blanked, but it was still an eventful start to the season!

My best fish from the Allen came later that season. On a bright, late summer day, I decided to have another crack at the river. I baited both of the main swims and wandered around looking for a bonus fish, but found none. After an hour I made my way back to the deep swim where there were the usual group of roach including the one that John had caught on opening day. This was now an easy fish to identify as the missing scales could be seen clearly in the water, showing up as a gold-speckled pattern on both sides. Further back in the swim *Esox* could be seen lurking amongst the weed. I made my way up to the other swim and saw four good roach moving in the cover of the bushes, picking maggots up as they passed through the gap. One of them looked as if it would make the 3lb mark.

I waited until the fish had moved back under the cover of the overhanging branches and then flicked a single swan shot link ledger into the gap. The hook was baited with two maggots and I positioned the rig so that I could see them. The roach moved back into the swim, with the larger fish masked behind the others. They picked up a few of the free offerings and then moved off. My bait had been moved, so it was possible that either one of the fish had picked it up or that a fish had moved the line on the way through. Minutes later the fish were back in, moving in the other direction. This time I saw one of the smaller fish pick up the bait, but I chose to ignore it. The fish continued their feeding pattern until all the maggots had been eaten. My hookbait apart from one pick-up remained unmolested.

I introduced more bait into the swim, and the roach continued moving back and forth eating bait on the way through. Then, after some half-hour or so, they came back into the swim and decided to stay. They ate most of the bait lying on the bottom, and again one of the smaller roach picked my bait up. I ignored it, and as it spat the bait from its mouth the larger roach took it before it had settled. This was it! I struck and made contact. As expected, the others all dashed for cover as the hooked fish fought in the gap amongst the bushes. I hustled it from under the upstream bush as it tried to follow its brethren, and with the fish then in the open the danger of losing it was greatly reduced. Less than a minute later it was on the bank. As I unhooked the fish and zeroed the scales I became convinced that the fish would make it to the 3lb mark. However, the needle settled just and only just short, and I had to settle for 2lb 15oz and a bit! This roach was extremely healthy, but actually slightly deformed. Well, that is not strictly fair: it had the same proportions as a three-pound roach until you looked beyond its dorsal fin. At this point the distance between the back of the dorsal and root of the tail was considerably shorter than it should have been. If this part of the fish had been in proportion to the front it would certainly have been well in excess of 3lb.

In all, I would say that including the fish lost to the large pike I had seen five roach over 3lb in this section of the Allen. I spent a few more chosen days on the Allen after this, going after the roach that it held. I caught a number of 2lb fish but never made it to the 3lb mark. The reason for this was that pollution once again reared its ugly head.

In the closed season of 1991, I was driving through Wimborne when I decided to have a look at the river where it follows a public footpath upstream from the middle of the town. Everywhere I looked there was a hand-written notice warning people to keep away and to stop pets from drinking from the river. These notices were signed by a woman police constable and were dated from the previous day. The first thing I did was to go to the nearby police station, but being Sunday it was closed. By the time I managed to track the WPC down, it was Monday morning. Inquiring as to what had occurred, I was told that a chemical of some sort had got into the river and fish had been seen floating dead down the river.

'Has it been reported to either the local angling club or the water authority?' I asked.

'No,' she replied.

'Have you made any attempt to find the source of the pollution?' I asked.

'No, the colour of the river was milky when I saw the fish floating down, but it soon cleared.'

I reported the matter myself to the Wessex Water Authority and the local angling club. Of course, there was little they could do after the delay, and yet again the polluters, whoever they were, got away with it. The River Allen coarse fish stocks have been set back and now there are very few fish left in the river at all. On a reconnaissance exercise a few days later and at intervals during the closed season I found very few coarse fish, and no grayling or trout whatsoever. I found the odd roach but these were not large, and were swimming with a few chub and some small dace. I did see the usual size brown trout and one or two pike later in the next season. All is not lost on the roach front, however, as some small shoals appeared towards the end of the 1991–2 season, presumably some of them having migrated from the River Stour. There are still no grayling showing as yet, but these may well appear from further upstream.

Perhaps in a few years' time the fish will once again flourish in this glorious small chalk-stream, but only time will tell. So, enough of the Allen and back on with the other Wessex rivers.

When fishing for other species such as chub and barbel, roach will often be on the hemp and corn before the barbel show. In visible waters this can be used to your advantage, but those anglers who believe roach to be shy fish had better not read the next paragraph.

Roach do not care about heavy line or large hooks. It is easy to pick off a roach or two when using these, simply by watching them take the bait and then striking. I have had a lot of fish on 8lb Kryston to a size 8 hook, and with two grains or corn finished on the drop. Now, if roach are tackle-shy as a lot of roach anglers would have us believe, why do they take baits presented in this way? One of my standard winter tactics these days when the river is clear is to fish with fixed 2oz feeders, an 18in tail with 8lb Kryston as hook length and 6lb maxima as main line. I know that many anglers will think that these are completely over-the-top tactics for roach, but read on . . .

The problem in these situations is fishing lighter would minimize the chances of landing a *Barbus maximus* should he decide to muscle in on the roach. Let's face it, the amount of large roach taken by anglers fishing for barbel with feeder maggots is high enough to justify the approach. For the record, the best fish I have had using this method was one at 3lb 1oz. In areas where there are no barbel, however, then I would drop down to 4lb line. As further illustration of this method's success, on one occasion while barbel fishing with a 3oz bolt rig with short tail size 4 hook and hair-rigged peanut, I had two roach which weighed in at a respectable 2lb 12oz and 2lb 10oz. The following night I fished with two rods, one on a bolt rig for the barbel, the other being a quivertip rod with 6lb line and 8lb Kryston terminated with a size 10 hook which was baited with a half-peanut. I caught two more roach both on the bolt rig, but never even raised a bite on the tip rod. On one particular gravel pit in my area the carp boys stopped using peanuts as there were too many roach in the water which were all too willing to hang themselves on the bolt rigs. So much for the shy roach!

Most of my roach fishing now fits into two main categories. The first is very much opportunist, as described earlier. During the summer months I now rarely, if ever, go out with roach in mind, but if I spot a good roach then I will have a go for it. My second approach is to pick my days during the winter months and to spend time actively fishing for roach. Although I prefer moving water, on occasion I have gone in search of roach at the odd stillwater and have had some successful days with the occasional 2lb fish to show for my efforts. Recently, I took my personal best roach of 3lb 6oz from a Hampshire gravel pit, the account of which now follows.

A Personal Best Stillwater Roach

I had been waiting for the conditions to be right on this gravel pit for about a month or so when on Sunday 1 December I thought that they were perfect – warm, overcast and with a slight breeze. I had done a bit of fish spotting on the lake over the previous weeks and had occasionally put a few maggots into a swim in which I had seen roach rolling. On arrival, I found the wind was coming across the lake straight in my direction and I set up the rods at the swim. The method I had decided on was 1½oz feeder fished as a confidence rig on one rod and a fixed feeder on the other, both at a distance of 25yd on to the clear gravel area.

An hour into the session I had a bite which turned out to be a tench of around 4lb, and then shortly after this another tench came to the net at around the same weight. Both of these fish had been taken on the fixed feeder. I then missed two bites – both on the fixed feeder – which resulted in squashed maggots and what looked suspiciously like roach bites. I changed both rods to confidence rigs and missed about four or five bites in the space of an hour. I am reasonably sure that roach were responsible. Then at 3.50 p.m. the left-hand monkey started to climb very slowly. Two bleeps out of the Optonic I hit it. The rod bent over and a good fish was thumping on the end – this was no tench. The fish kited away to the left and was brought in fighting all the way. As the fish neared the bank I saw it and it was obvious that it was a good 3lb one.

My first attempt at bringing it over the net saw the fish bolt off back out again – I have never had to back-wind on a roach before, but this fish gave me no choice. The second time I got it back it just slid straight into the net. When it was safely on the bank and I had removed the hook, I zeroed the scales and slipped the fish into the sling. It was a new personal best at 3lb 6oz. I sacked the fish and went to collect my camera gear, and once I had sorted it out and checked the light meter I realized that I would need the flash. I switched on the flash gun and nothing happened. I then spent the next hour driving around garages to find some new batteries, and eventually found some at an extortionate price. Perhaps I should take more notice of the good information I have given in the Introduction.

Once loaded, the flash worked perfectly and the fish was taken from the sack, and then returned to the pit after being witnessed and photographed. I did not feel that it was worth fishing on any longer as it was quite dark by then. If I had remembered the batteries in the first place then who knows? Perhaps I would have had another one.

Back to river roach fishing. Generally, the time for the best roach fishing is after the river has been up for a while and is starting to thin out a bit, or when a warm spell follows a lengthy cold one. These are times when you are in with the best chance of a decent return for your efforts.

Baits should generally be either bread if the river still has any colour left in it or maggots if it has not. There are times when other baits will work and these are often worth a try, particularly during the summer but less so in the winter. What about methods for catching big roach? Well, until recently I would have said that ledgering was the best method if you are after big river roach. Having had two 3lb fish near the end of the 1990–1 season and another in the 1991–2 season on the float, however, I would now say that it makes no difference. To be fair, I suppose the method you choose depends upon conditions on the day. I am certainly no purist when it comes to roach fishing and do not much care what line strength, bait or method I use so long as it catches fish!

The breakdown in methods and baits for the six 3lb river roach I have taken is as follows: quivertip bread, one fish at 3lb 1oz; float-fished bread, two fish at 3lb 3oz and 3lb; fixed-feeder maggot, one fish at 3lb 1oz (on 6lb line and 8lb Kryston hook length); float-fished maggot, one fish at 3lb 5oz; quivertip sweetcorn, one fish at 3lb 1oz.

Two of the 3lb 1oz fish were caught on the Dorset Stour while the other four threes were caught on the Hampshire Avon. My only roach

A perfect 3lb 6oz fish glows through the dark.

over 3lb from a stillwater came on maggot in conjunction with a 1½oz feeder fished on a confidence rig. All but one of the roach (which is mentioned) were caught on 4lb line!

These statistics prove absolutely nothing to me but I dare say that someone can make something of them. One thing I will say is that I have taken more 3lb roach from the Avon that I have from the Stour, although the Stour seems to produce more roach of all sizes. It has only been in recent years that the Avon has started to produce any amount of small roach – I wonder if the reduction in weed cutting on the Avon over the last few years has got anything to do with this? Certainly there are more young fish (roach in particular) in the Avon now than there have been in the last few seasons.

There are many various reasons for the decline in the amount of fish on the Avon. One reason that seems to be overlooked is that in years gone by, the Avon was bordered by water meadows for most of its length. These were worked and controlled by the various keepers along its banks. I can recall a time in my youth when the upper reaches of the Avon around the Salisbury area had extensive water meadows both above and below the city. These water meadows held an awful lot of food and fish, and I can recall fishing in the main carriers and below the hatches that fed the meadows themselves. Grayling, trout, dace, small chub and roach were all in abundance. A lot of the fry would migrate into the meadows for the early part of their lives before moving into the main river. Some of the actual spawning took place in the entrances to the larger carriers, and the small fry had an excellent nursery area in which to grow. These spawning and growing areas have now gone, and very few of these water meadows exist anywhere on the Avon. In the areas where they do still exist, the population of fish is generally higher than anywhere else on the river.

Sadly, the water meadows that have been lost are now gone forever. The water levels on the Avon are a lot lower than they were in the past, and weirs on the Avon do not really exist as they once did. The controlling hatches that still remain are left wide open at the slightest hint of rain, thereby allowing the water to speed its way to the sea. They often stay that way as no one ever seems to bother closing them again. It seems that the only time they are closed is when the salmon make their way upstream. The reason for this is that it keeps them in the stretch for that much longer as the only way up is through the ladder or up the sill itself.

With salmon on the Avon being less plentiful than they once were, every stretch tries to contain them as long as possible. However, it would be a major boost to the Avon if the controllers of the weirs on the river used them in the way for which they were first designed. The levels would then be higher and some of the carriers would once again have water in them – the chance of these all containing water are once again virtually nil. Most of the hatches are now beyond repair and the cost of replacing them would be vast. A lot of the carriers themselves are now little more than depressions in the ground and to restore them they would have to be dug out, again at more expense. The financial justification of any such project would be low as the only people to benefit would be the anglers, bird-watchers and wildfowlers. Consequently, the water meadows now remain just a memory for some, while for others they never even existed. The combination of lower water levels and water volume, extensive weed cutting and the decline of the water meadows have all played a part in the decline of the Avon. There are, no doubt, also many other contributing factors. Yet the Avon still rates as one of the finest rivers in Britain, despite the problems it has suffered.

And as for records? Well I for one am certain that there are roach over 4lb in both the Avon and the Stour. Ray Clarke managed to get one of them from the Stour, a magnificent fish of 4lb 3oz which now holds the British record. This was from one of those places that does not yield too many roach, but when one does get caught it is a good one. Most people were surprised at Ray's fish and a lot of anglers were also very jealous, making rather puerile remarks to me about it. One roach angler thought that Ray did not deserve the fish as he had never even caught a 2lb roach before. My reply? 'So what! He was fishing for big roach and he got one!'

I do not think that Ray's record is by any means a safe one, however, as either river could produce another leviathan – I know as I have seen them swimming around. A lot of rich stillwaters with low-density populations of roach are also more than capable of producing a new record. In one such water that for obvious reasons shall remain nameless, a roach measuring 18½in with a girth of 15in was found dead at the beginning of the 1991–2 season. It was not weighed as it had started to decompose, but I think that is is reasonably safe to assume that it weighed over 4lb when alive. Only one big roach needs to make one mistake for the record to fall again.

Terry Lampard's super shot of Ray Clarke's 4lb 3oz record.

8

Grayling

The grayling was one of the first fish I ever caught, and I took it from the River Itchen just above Bishopstoke. I was about eight years old at the time and was guesting. As I said earlier, at that age and in those days you could get away with it. These days, however, my grayling fishing has to be done on club waters or on day tickets. In Wessex and the surrounding area there is easy access to a lot of waters that have some really excellent fishing for this species.

In the Wessex area such waters include the middle to upper reaches of the Hampshire Avon, the Nadder, the Wylye, middle reaches of the Dorset Stour and the Frome (along with some of their tributaries), and, until recently the tiny River Allen. Further afield, the River Test, River Itchen and River Kennet hold some tremendous stocks of grayling, including some very worthwhile fish. A lot of the lakes and gravel pits in this area also hold them, providing that they are fed by the rivers. Even river-fed lakes and pits that have been stocked only rarely turn into very good waters. Lakes that are not fed by rivers do not hold viable stocks of grayling. The reason for this is that grayling demand clean, highly oxygenated water and few lakes that are not fed by streams or that are not endowed with heavy springs can provide the high demands that the fish need. The lakes and gravel pits that do hold grayling, however, often contain fish of exceptional size, those topping 3lb being caught regularly.

I shall deal with the Wessex rivers first, and will start with the Hampshire Avon. The Avon has a good head of grayling and fish over 2lb are caught throughout the river, along with the occasional three-pounder – most of these are from the middle to upper sections. The lower river today has very few grayling, but the odd fish does show up every now and again. The Severals Fishery was once an excellent place to catch grayling but there are not too many of them around now. In fact, it is only in very recent years that they have started to show up at all. Whether this has got anything to do with recent stockings on stretches upstream, I am not sure, but it stands to reason that at least some of the present stocks are from this source. Once above the town of Ringwood, the fish gradually increase in numbers the further up the river you go. They are very much a headwater fish and so most of the stocked fish gradually migrate up toward Salisbury.

Once above the city itself, access becomes somewhat restricted on the Avon. Most of the upper river is designated to fly fishing, some being under club control with the lion's share belonging to Salisbury and District Angling Club. You have to pay an increased member-ship fee for these stretches to take into account the price of stocking brown trout which is, I believe, a more than fair condition. While this ruling may not suit those who intend to fish for grayling only, it does work extremely well for the club in that it means that a guaranteed amount of cash is available at the start of the trout season rather that the club having to anticipate revenue to cover stockings. Anyway, any grayling enthusiast should consider paying this increase because the stocks of fish in these areas are far higher than those on any other part of the river. The Wylye, Nadder and Bourne are also included on the Salisbury ticket, with some sections being covered under the same conditions.

The Stour is almost entirely controlled by clubs and, as they are geared toward the coarse angler, the access is far greater. Unfortunately, the fishing is not as productive as on the Avon, and the fish are difficult to find. The bonus is that if you can find them then 3lb fish are definitely on the cards, although 2lb ones are more likely. The Stour is totally different from the Avon as far as grayling are concerned. The only areas likely to contain any viable stocks of grayling are in the middle reaches from around the Wimborne area up to Blandford. Most of these are provided from stockings of unwanted coarse fish from the preserved trout-only stretches of the upper Avon, Nadder and Wylye. Most of these trout-only stretches are electro-fished at the end of each trout season to remove all coarse fish. However, whether the grayling is a coarse fish or, as its adipose fin suggests, a member of the salmon family, is open to question. While fly-fishing purists would have you believe it is the former and should be removed with the other coarse fish, textbooks say it is a salmonoid. So where does that leave the grayling? Out on a limb, I'm afraid!

The River Frome probably has the best grayling fishing in Britain. The amount of fish over 3lb is amazing, 2lb fish are common and fish in the 1–2lb range are found virtually throughout the river up to Dorchester. Above this town there do not appear to be any grayling – at least, not yet! The Frome holds the record for grayling, with an exceptional fish weighing 4lb 3oz. This fish was caught in 1989 by Mr S. Lanigan late in the season, truly a fabulous fish and great achievement, beating my record by nearly ½lb. The coarse fishing access, however, is very limited on this river – you cannot get on most of the water before the end of the salmon season, and even then the amount of available fishing is small. There are some huge fish on this river, and if only we coarse anglers could get more access I am sure the grayling record would be bettered.

The grayling is not an indigenous species to the Frome and was introduced by, would you believe it, one of the purist trout fishing clubs! As the Frome is subject to the same policy of coarse fish removal as any other trout-only water, you may find this rather surprising. The fact is, that in the past the River Frome was seriously polluted by chemicals. This wiped out all of the fish stocks, coarse and game, for some distance downstream of Wool. The only fish that did survive were those in the side-streams and carriers. The controlling bodies on this stretch of river had no trout left to fish for, but were loath to reintroduce them in case they could not survive or would move to other stretches. The food chain was also virtually wiped out by the same pollution.

A compromise was made when the local water authority offered to stock the water with grayling from, I believe, the upper reaches of the Avon and its tributaries. This was deemed to be a good idea as grayling are very closely associated with the needs of brown trout in that they demand a similar diet and the same high oxygen levels. The grayling, being regarded as expendable, were to be the guinea-pigs. The clubs, meanwhile wrongly assumed that they would be able to remove the grayling within a few weeks if the water proved to be suitable for restocking with trout.

However, the introduced grayling departed from the stretch within days of being stocked, the availability of food being so scarce that they went in all directions in search of sustenance. So, there you have it. The worst enemy of the dedicated trout angler was introduced by the very same people that now fight a losing battle in eradicating the species from the southern chalk-streams!

The grayling record is, I am reasonably sure, beaten by trout anglers on the Frome every year. As an illustration of why these are not claimed, the rules governing one particular water state that anyone who claims a record or reports any large fish to the press will be removed from the club. Personally, I find this most distasteful as I know that most of these fish are thrown into bankside vegetation and left to rot. What a total waste of such a sporting and highly edible fish.

As I have made a reference to grayling as an edible fish, I feel that I must quantify this. Grayling are regarded by many as being far nicer than trout in terms of taste. I whole-heartedly agree with this and I, having eaten an immense amount of both, would say that the grayling beats the trout hands down for both taste and texture. What I am about to say may well cost me a small amount of fishing on a certain stretch of river should the keeper decide to read this book, but I will say it anyway!

One way that you can acquire winter fishing on some prime stretches of grayling river at no cost whatsoever is to offer your services to help remove grayling from the trout-only stretches. Grayling are an extremely prolific species – you only have to look at any book written by a trout angler to realize this fact – and any reference to coarse fish will invariably cause fly fisherman to target the grayling as public enemy number one, coming even above the dreaded pike. The reason for this is that the grayling, being closely linked with the trout, is charged as the fish most likely to deprive the trout of its food supply. If it occurs in sufficient numbers, the grayling is also attributed with being able actually to drive trout from the stretch. Electro-fishing has proved to be an inadequate way of removing all the grayling from a water, and the fact is that, once established, it is impossible to remove grayling altogether. Now, it is obviously going against the grain for most self-respecting coarse anglers to remove any fish wantonly from a water, but wouldn't it be nice to have a stretch of water – in which the possibility of catching some very good fish exists – all to yourself for the winter months?

The way to go about this is that once you have offered your grayling-culling services, actually kill some of the smaller grayling and deliver them to the keeper for his tea, but return all the larger fish. This does not deprive the river of its adult fish stocks that have escaped the attention of the DC prods, and ensures that there will still be grayling in the stretch the following year. The coarse angler can in some way justify this approach to himself or herself as a lot of these grayling would otherwise be destined for 'death row'. The small amount of grayling that coarse fishermen remove is nothing when compared to the wanton destruction they will be subjected to at the beginning and end of the trout season!

Until recently, the river Allen held some wonderful fishing, the grayling record of 3lb 10oz being taken just upstream of Wimborne in 1983. I have had fish up to 2lb 14oz from the river and taken a lot of other 2lb fish over the years. Now, sadly, the river is more or less lacking in all species due to the amount of pollution that periodically leaked into the river. The only viable fish population that exists there now is the trout as these are introduced to provide sport for game fishermen. As I talked about the Allen in depth in the previous chapter, I will not dwell on it any longer here.

The River Itchen provides some excellent grayling fishing along its entire length, apart from at its head waters. It is a typical chalk-stream with lots of *Ranunculus* beds and exceptionally clear water. The river itself is fast flowing, and fish spotting is very much to the fore. Much of my youth was spent on this river and the lessons I learned there are still an invaluable asset in my present-day approach. In my misguided youth I ate the vast majority of the fish that I caught from this river, but the only time I would contemplate killing a fish for the table now is as described earlier.

The lowest reaches of the Itchen in the Swathling environs are free-fishing areas. At this point the river changes dramatically in the space of a couple of miles or so. From upstream of the road bridge just below the White Swan public house, the river is fast and generally shallow – this is the section where the best grayling fishing can be found. Once below the bridge, the pace of the water slows considerably before it falls through the hatches into the tidal waters below Woodmill. There are some good roach, dace and chub to be taken from this stretch, but for the grayling angler it holds little interest.

After leaving this stretch and following it as it winds its way toward its source, there is no coarse fishing whatsoever until the town of Bishopstoke is reached. The coarse fishing at this point is under club control and extends to just above and below the town, and access is mainly limited to after the end of the salmon season. Then, once again, the majority of the remaining river is strictly preserved for game fishing, although there is a limited amount of fishing available in the city of Winchester, again free of charge. There are some day ticket trout waters along the River Itchen, and while these are very pricey, they do offer the chance of catching some bonus grayling for those who are prepared to pay. I am not suggesting that you pay the price just to fish for grayling but, for those amongst us who do the odd day's fishing for trout during the closed season to relieve the boredom, they are there.

The River Test also offers some very useful fishing. Once again, while primarily a game river, some stretches do offer limited access to coarse fishermen. The stretch under the control of Ringwood and District Anglers' Association offers 1½ miles of double-bank fishing from November through to the start of the salmon season in February. This stretch runs from a point just up from the M27 where the bottom boundary of the fishery is situated. There are restrictions imposed to protect the salmon which must be adhered to strictly, and any trout – of which there are many – must be returned. While the temptation to take the odd trout home is there for some, it must be remembered that this could lose some valuable fishing for the club, and anyone doing so would not be looked upon too kindly by the other members!

The middle and upper reaches of the River Kennet have some immense grayling stocks, but it has now been some years since I first became acquainted with this picturesque Berkshire chalk river. My first trips were mostly aimed at the barbel it contains, but the magic of the grayling was enough of a draw to see me making the odd trip in the depths of winter in order to catch the 'lady of the stream'. One of the most delightful waters I have ever had the good fortune to fish must be the Craven Estate high up the river. The fishing on this estate is geared towards trout anglers, but after 1 October it opens its doors to coarse fishing. As well as reasonably large grayling, there are some excellent roach to be caught from the water. Trout, of course, are extremely evident and can prove to be difficult to avoid.

The author holds the impossible! A brace of 3lb grayling.

The river at this point drops through the Kennet and Avon Canal. Both the canal and part of the top section of the river are navigable, but this is not the most pleasing part of the river's stretch. Once the river drops down from the canal it becomes very shallow and overgrown – just as nature intended. This small section is where most of the grayling are to be found, and it is also very pleasing to the eye. As with most chalk-streams, the grayling here are easily seen and spooked but, with a careful approach, they may be caught. I have taken as many as twenty fish in a day from this water, and the largest I caught is a fish of 2lb 8oz – by no means a monster, but a good fish none the less.

More recently, I was invited by Andy Holland to fish the Kennet lower down the river below Newbury. This section of the Kennet is very picturesque, being one of the longest stretches of natural, untouched regions on the river. The day's fishing, however, turned out to be a disaster!

We arrived at the stream at about 9 a.m., only to find a deluge in progress. With spotting out of the question, Andy decided on an early-lunch-come-late-breakfast, and made eggs and bacon in the fishing hut. In the corner there were a couple of pieces of angling history: an old black and white photo of the famous Ibsley barbel of 16lb 1oz, being displayed by the late Colonel Crow; and Dick Walker's bait kettle. After breakfast the rain eased slightly and we ventured out to look at the river. In no time at all it had risen and had a tinge of colour – there was not much chance of a grayling that day.

Andy makes breakfast as the rain falls.

Still, we tried. I managed one fish on the day – a very small chub of about 2oz that took a heavily leaded nymph. By mid-afternoon the weather had closed in again and all our enthusiasm for continuing had gone. We spent the next hour or so in the hut waiting for the rain to ease, but it was not to be. Still, it was enjoyable just the same and I look forward to being able to catch a brace or two of grayling from this delightful stretch in the future.

The 'stillwaters' in the area are varied and well spread. Probably the most famous of these was Loudsmill near Dorchester which in some ways was unique. At one time it was fed by the Frome and for some time was a trout fishery. The trout-fishery owner then allowed a tackle business to take control of the lake and to run it on a day-ticket basis for coarse fishing. The proprietor of the tackle shop had the foresight to introduce into the lake around forty or so grayling that would otherwise have been killed after electro-fishing on a very short section of the Frome. These fish went in at up to 3lb 8oz – incidentally, this gives a very good indication of what one might expect grayling to attain on the Frome. With few trout left in the lake by this time, the grayling found themselves in a very rich water with little competition for the available food supply and therefore thrived. This water was situated just at the upper limit of the grayling encroachment on the Frome and, as the small feeder stream that skirted the lake contained a few grayling, it is possible that some fish were already present before the introduction of the Frome fish – this, however, is open to conjecture. During the next year the introduced fish packed on weight and the lake became well known for its big grayling.

After reading about the lake in the *Angling Times* I decided to investigate it myself. From the reports on the water the potential of a British record seemed very probable, and several visits later I caught a couple of fish over 2lb. The lake was by no means an easy water and the resident grayling would often prove extremely fickle. Some of the fish that I saw during evenings at the lake as they rose to take the abundant fly life seemed to be very close to, if not exceeding, the record at the time. At this time several fish had been taken over 3lb, but I did not know how many of these were recaptures.

After several more visits to the water I was lucky enough to hook and land a 3lb 12oz which was later accepted as a record. I had to resort to very fine line to get any bites at all from the fish, and was not at all confident of landing any on such light tackle. I am almost sure that the chances of landing such a fish would have been remote should it have been in running water. Shortly after the capture of this fish, another which was only 1oz lower in weight was caught. The angler concerned showed me a photograph of this fish and it appeared to be the same one, although I am not totally sure of this as the way that the fish was held did not allow positive identification. From later evidence it seems that there were at least four different grayling over 3lb in weight in this water. One photograph of a fish of 3lb 6oz has proved to be the same fish I caught at 3lb 12oz. This was taken some three months before my capture and appears to be the only definite other landing of this particular fish.

Sadly, all these grayling have now perished. The tackle dealer closed the shop due to lack of business and gave up control of the lake during the following closed season. The controlling hatch that fed the lake soon became blocked. As the vital flow of water had become restricted, oxygen levels fell and the grayling could no longer survive.

Other lakes and pits also containing grayling are not so well known, and it is worth checking out any water that is in the immediate vicinity of a known grayling river. I am sure that Loudsmill was not the only water capable of containing fish above the present record, and most trout lakes in the area that are fed by rivers with stocks of grayling also seem to hold them. Indeed, I have spent many an hour trying to catch grayling instead of rainbows, and Dever Springs is a prime example of one such water. The tiny River Dever has some tremendous stocks of quality grayling. These have infiltrated the top lake in particular, and can often be seen feeding on nymphs near the point where the feeder enters and the overflow exits the lake.

Anyway, enough of the location of grayling in the rivers I have fished, and on to methods of capture.

Techniques and Tactics

By far the easiest way to catch grayling in numbers is to float fish for them. The best baits in order of my preference are maggot, worm and sweetcorn. Worms suitable for grayling are either small reds or brandling. Lobworms will take fish, but in general they are too large to be of much use – although the tail or head of a lob can be used if no other bait is available. This method of fishing is non-selective but is very productive. Obviously, good fish will come your way when you use this method, and in any case due to depth it is often the only way to fish certain stretches.

Grayling will feed in all conditions although coloured water seems to produce very few fish, the reason for this being that they are primarily sight feeders. You can catch fish in any depth of water and at any level – they will take a bait a foot from the surface in deep water, right on the bottom and anywhere between. Faster runs will produce lots of fish of all sizes while bigger fish generally prefer the steadier flow, although there are no guarantees of this. They can and do often turn up in the white water below hatches and weirs, or along fast, shallow runs. Spotting the fish in swims such as these is nigh on impossible and there is only one way to find out if any fish are in residence: fish all the swims methodically.

One location that is often completely overlooked is on small feeder streams that enter a river system. These waters are hardly, if ever, fished at all, but grayling are very adept at colonizing such small streams and carriers. While spotting in these carriers is relatively easy, these fish can prove extremely difficult to catch. The streams may be little more than fast-flowing ditches, and so fish in these areas are easily spooked as they are unlikely to have seen any bankside movement at all – apart from the odd cow. The problem is further aggravated by the fact that the only way of presenting a bait in these situations is to use a single shot on the line and to guide the bait to where the fish is situated. This is easy enough when there is plenty of room in which to work, but it is no mean feat when the bankside vegetation is totally against you. The solution to this problem is to approach these waters in a completely different way when in search of good fish.

There is no point in creeping along the banks of such streams with the intention of spotting fish and catching them on the same day. This method may work, but the time spent trying to coax fish from these waters after you have spooked them can be put to far better use. Instead, make your way along the bank while adopting a high profile. Each decent fish that you spot should be logged and the bank marked with something suitable. Any vegetation that will directly interfere with presentation can then be trimmed back in each swim. I hasten to add here that I am not advocating the wanton destruction of bankside trees or branches as this is neither conductive nor necessary to catching grayling, or indeed any other fish. Any branches that need to be moved can easily be tied back temporarily to enable you to cast. Once you have completed these tasks you can fish on the main rivers or carriers for the remainder of the day, and then return to these small streams the following day. By this time grayling will have returned to their station and will offer a much better chance of capture. Once you have moved through the water and caught some of these fish, it is simple to remove the ties from the branches so that the vegetation is much as it was before.

On the main river and carriers a good way of catching big fish is also to look for them first. They can be difficult to spot, as they blend in very well with the bottom of the river bed. One way to combat this spotting problem is to introduce a few maggots to the chosen swim and then watch as the grayling move to intercept them in the current. This method will soon tell you if there are fish in the swim as they show themselves readily – providing that you are reasonably still and quiet in your approach, and, of course, that they are feeding. If visibility is really good you will be able to pick out the biggest fish by sight as you watch it take the bait. This is easy in steady water, but anywhere else you will just have to go through the motions.

When walking the banks you may be fortunate enough to spot a solitary big fish. If it is already feeding on passing insect life it can soon be persuaded to take a maggot. If the fish does not appear to be feeding and cannot be coaxed into taking maggot, a well-placed worm ledgering on the bottom and slightly upstream of the fish will often produce a bite. This method of spotting will often allow you to pick out individual fish without having to put any bait in at all – particularly so if you see the fish hard on the bottom nymphing. Roving around throughout the day will catch more fish than if you sit in one swim all the time.

Of course, if you do spot a big fish then by all means spend some time going after it, but if it does not take a bait after an hour then the chances are that is is not going to be tempted to feed. The grayling is by nature a very territorial fish and will not move far from its chosen swim – even when spooked by a clumsy footfall or when a shadow is cast over it, the fish will soon return. While it is possible to catch some of these fish on the same day that you spot them, should this fail then you can always return the following day and have another attempt in the knowledge that the fish will be there.

Unfortunately, the grayling is a very unpredictable fish. One day such a fish will not be tempted into taking anything, while the next it will be feeding voraciously. It is worth illustrating this point here by recounting the events of a couple of days I spent on the River Allen some years ago.

I had spent a day on the river and although I had found a few fish I could not get them to feed. The following day I fished elsewhere in the morning and then dropped in on the Allen around midday. I met a friend coming off the water and he told me that he had taken a few grayling, including two of 2lb with the best at 2lb 11oz. I thought that this was probably one of the fish I had been after the day before, but decided to have a look anyway.

I made straight for the swim and found the grayling happily feeding on passing grubs and the like. I threw in a few maggots and the grayling managed to get all of them, even darting downstream to get the last one before returning to its station. It then took my bait on the first cast and weighed in at 2lb 11oz. Happy with this result, I left the water. It was not until some days later that, while having a drink with friends, I discovered that a third grayling of the same weight had been taken later in the same afternoon. It seemed too much of a coincidence that they were different fish as we had all caught them in the same small area, and on comparing photos later it did indeed turn out to be the same one!

This is by no means an isolated incident. I once hooked a grayling that I had spotted on the middle Avon, but after a short fight it snapped me and I thought that that was it. An hour later I returned to the swim. The fish was back and took a grain of sweetcorn that I threw in. I trotted another grain through the swim a couple of feet off the bottom and the fish rose up to intercept it. After a quick strike the fish was hooked and landed this time, the hook and a short length of line with split shot still to be seen hanging from its mouth after the earlier fight. So you see, sometimes they literally give themselves up.

The top fish went to 1lb 12oz, and the bottom a fabulous 3lb 1oz.

The other method of catching grayling, but one which is not so popular with coarse anglers, is to fish for them with a fly rod. You can really gain some valuable fishing using this method as a lot of clubs have waters that are trout only at reasonable day ticket or annual price, sometimes even free. The restrictions are usually that upstream nymph and dry fly may be used only. You will find grayling as well as trout in these waters because, as illustrated earlier, the conditions that suit trout also suit grayling. Because most clubs remove grayling and other coarse fish from these trout waters there are not so many of these fish about, but the ones that are tend to be big. These grayling will rise to virtually any fly on some days, and will accept nymphs readily if they are not feeding on the surface. I have found that the best nymph by far is a shrimp pattern.

It may therefore be well worth your while investing in a fly rod and paying the day ticket charge to have a go. The charge for a day's fishing will also include a brace or two of trout, but bear in mind that you should leave these until last as once they are taken it is usual for fishing to cease. In all, it is very satisfying to catch grayling on a fly, and it is also nice to have a section of river to yourself for a day.

To summarize, the grayling can be caught on most days and in most conditions. What other fish can be caught in freezing weather, brilliant sunshine or on the most miserable overcast and rainy day, and at any time during the day? Perhaps the chub is nearly as accommodating, but you try spooking one of them and see if it will then take a bait!

9

Delightful Diversions

Dace

This is a fish that is looked upon with mixed feelings. For some it is only worthwhile as a bait fish, for others it is a good fish to make up the weights in match fishing, and for a few it is regarded as a worthy specimen. Most anglers (myself included) who use dace for bait fish can, still appreciate the capture of a good specimen and limit the size of fish taken as bait. For example, pike anglers like myself would not dream of using a 1lb dace for bait. During the course of a season on the Avon it is not unusual for anglers to catch quite a few fish around this mark, and in the 1991–2 season I had five dace of 1lb or more in weight. A 1lb dace makes an impressive sight to behold, and I am sure that the Avon holds fish in excess of the present record. Few anglers realize just how heavy a dace is as large fish of exactly the same length can have completely different weights, depending on whether they are male or female fish.

During the latter part of the season in particular, dace will shoal up in certain areas of the Avon. These shoals are quite literally massive; for example, a dace shoal of several thousand fish was seen on the Somerly Estate during the mid 1980s. I would say that this was not an over exaggeration as shoals of this size are often found late in the season when they group prior to spawning. The spots in which these numbers of fish can be found are well known to pleasure anglers, practising match anglers and those seeking bait fish.

One such a spot on the Avon receives the attention of many anglers around the Christmas period, when the dace really start to show up in numbers. From then on, pike anglers and pike gather to make good use of these natural larders. Pleasure and match anglers often take bags approaching 100lb in a day, and this is not just limited to one angler who happens to be on the fish – often these weights will be taken by two or more anglers on a given day with a lot of back-up weights besides. This continues right up until the end of the season.

These two dace are almost exactly the same length and yet the bottom fish (at 15oz) is 3oz heavier than the top fish.

Very few of the fish caught by these anglers are, weighed, because they come to the net so fast the angler becomes completely taken up with catching the next fish. On one occasion when I needed some bait for my intended day's pike fishing, one of the anglers I knew offered me a few fish to use. When we lifted out his net I remarked that some of the dace looked as if they weighed a pound or so. He admitted that he had not taken much notice of the fish as he was catching one on every cast. We weighed three fish that looked slightly larger than the rest: one weighed 15oz and the other two went at 1lb 1oz each. Now if

The Hampshire Avon at Bisterne.

157

this angler did not realize the size of the fish he caught – and to be fair, as a match angler he should have done – how many others over a pound just get returned at the end of each day?

Dace can be a very demanding fish. Often I have gone out with the intention of pike fishing, only to be sidetracked by dace coming so fast that I have become completely absorbed in catching them. When I finally realize what the time is I often do not have enough daylight left for the pike.

Dace can, however, also be a very accommodating fish. There are few days when they will not feed should you be able to find them. They hold no great mystique and are easily caught. The only time they seem to be put off the feed is when the odd prowling pike appears. Providing that you are armed with the appropriate tackle at such a time, it is easy enough to use one of the dace to catch the pike so that you can move it upstream somewhere should it prove too trouble-some. This may catch you a bonus large pike as well!

Dace can be found almost anywhere during the season, spread thinly all through the river. Only during the pre-spawning period will you find them in any great numbers, and the rest of the time they will usually be in year-class groups. Should you catch one dace of around a pound from such a group, stick with it as it is likely that you will catch other very similar sized fish.

In all, it seems a shame that the dace is so much an underrated fish, as no doubt the record is out there to be caught. This is not only true of the Avon as the Stour and many other rivers in Britain also hold good dace. I often wonder if anglers are embarrassed to claim a dace record as I am sure they are with gudgeon. Take it from me, should I catch either I will claim a record! British records are not there just to provide the captor with his or her moment of glory; they are there as historic fact that a given species can attain a particular weight in British waters. While I write this book, an angler has claimed the gudgeon record whilst another has taken a dace of 1lb 5oz, choosing not to make a claim.

Carp

While baiting swims on the river in the summer months I often find fish that I am not really intending to fish for at the time. Amongst others, these can include roach, tench, carp and often some very good pike. I leave the pike unmolested unless I have to catch them and move them away from the swim so that I can continue fishing, although I do

record their position if I think they will be of interest to me in the winter months. The other species, however, are often well worth catching, and I will deal with carp in this section.

Carp on the Rivers Avon and Stour are like the rest of the species this river holds – big! There are a lot of fish in these rivers in the 20lb plus bracket, with the odd fish weighing over 30lb. The Royalty in particular holds an awful lot of carp, many of them well in excess of 20lb and with the Parlour Pool in particular holding many. These can be induced to take bread crust from the surface, particularly during the closed season when you can get an idea of the size potential you can expect. Many of the so-called big barbel that anglers lose on these rivers after a short battle – when the unseen quarry belts off at an alarming rate and snaps 6lb line like cotton – are probably actually river carp. The carp in the Avon and Stour are widespread, and at times will move into an area that an angler has baited with hemp and corn in order to attract barbel. These carp seem generally to appear in groups of fish rather than as individuals, and their weights can vary from single-figure fish up to large twenties. As mentioned earlier, although 30lb fish are not common they do occasionally make an appearance, but even then are not often caught. Again, they are usually found in the company of others. The first genuine thirty that I know of from the Avon was recently reported to the angling press – this was a mirror carp from the Royalty.

The author's best river common carp.

These fish are often very easy to catch, including the larger ones. Most of the fish will have never seen the bank before and if caution is used when casting, then the fish are often very obliging. Approaching them rather like barbel, the bigger fish can be singled out from the rest. I have found that by using a rig that does not hook the fish or panic it so that it tears off with the bait in its mouth, it will not show any alarm and you can choose which fish you want. The rig I employ is a simple link ledger of no more than two swan shot. The hook length is around 2ft, with a size 6 hook to which 1in or so of hair is tied from the bend. To this I attach two or three grains of corn. It is an easy rig to eject if ever there was one!

The carp will feed freely on any free offerings you throw in, and it does not matter how much you put in as they will eat the lot. All that I do then is place the bait in a position where I can see it easily and wait to see what happens. If luck is with me, the biggest fish may be the first to pick up the bait; if it is not then I do nothing – the hook is soon ejected, usually with the corn still on the hair. As soon as the fish I am after picks the bait up, a controlled strike is all that is needed to set the hook. Then all hell breaks loose!

As the carp are not used to being caught, they will take off in any direction as fast as possible. As I know what I am up against, I lose very few fish as the pressure I apply from the start does not allow the fish to get up too much speed – the amount of restraint that can be exerted using 6lb line, barbel rod and pin is quite considerable. The fight between you and the carp has to be kept in your favour at all times, because if the carp gets its head, it may take you considerable time to regain control of the situation and the fish may be lost. Although I am not a carp angler I do enjoy catching these fish. My best wild, common and mirror carp have all come from the rivers and weighed 9lb 8oz, 21lb 14oz and 24lb 15oz respectively.

There are those who object strongly to the presence of carp in both the Avon and Stour, and more so the Avon it seems. Most of the objections come from the barbel anglers. Although these carp should in fact not really be there, finding their way as they do into the rivers when nearby lakes become flooded, it must be remembered that neither should the barbel! Their introduction produced much the same reaction from the roach anglers. The fact is that the carp are here to stay and are getting bigger. It may even be the case that these river carp will carry on to become well worth the effort of the carp angler's attentions. Meanwhile, I will continue to enjoy catching green carp.

How about this for a river carp? The author's best.

Tench

I am mainly interested in river fishing, and although there are a fair number of tench in the Rivers Stour and Avon (including some quite large fish), they are few and far between. In this section I will therefore deal with river tench last, and recount my limited encounters with stillwater tench first.

Stillwater Tench Fishing

Tench fishing in the last few years has changed dramatically. The target weight for a specimen fish these days has got to be over 8lb, with fish into double figures regarded as *the* fish to catch. This is far removed from my earlier tench fishing days in the 1970s when fish over 5lb were rare. When I first went back to catching tench I started out using a float and maggot. Although I did catch a few fish in the first couple of days, it became obvious that the carp anglers on the water were also catching tench and these were of a larger average size than the fish I had been taking. Although I had already beaten my then personal best by over a pound with a fish of 6lb 6oz, they were taking fish of 7lb and more. I cannot give any exact weights here as it seems usual for carp anglers to regard them as 'nuisance' fish and just throw them back. I find it a sad state of affairs when good fish are treated with contempt because anglers become blinkered toward other successes. I myself am not without blame here, as during my 'barbel-only period' I treated chub in much the same way. Anyway, back to the tench and it was not long before I realized that I would get better results if I adopted a similar approach to the carp anglers.

The methods and tackle used these days when in pursuit of tench bear no resemblance to the float fishing or feeder fishing that I have used in the past. These days it is very much a case of boilies and hair rigs used in conjunction with rods in excess of 1¼lb test curve, line strengths over 7lb and bait runners. The reason for this change to what is basically light carp fishing gear and methods is that tench have now grown to a larger average size. The very fact that boilies are being used – often over a bed of flavoured hemp, tares, maples and the like – will mean that, should they be there, carp will inevitably show in the swim sometime during your stay on the chosen venue. In fact, carp can cause a lot of problems when they do turn up. In the last few years I have fished for tench during the first weeks of the season up until spawning times. During this time, the carp are often the first fish to appear in the swim. While I do not mind the odd 20lb carp now and again, they have often come to the swim *en masse*, mopping up vast quantities of bait before the tench have had time to get in amongst my offerings.

The problem has been that once the carp get to know that food is readily available, they are prone to move in at anytime, day or night, and eat the lot. This means that you do not really know whether bait that you introduce one night will still be there when first light arrives. If you catch a carp during the hours of darkness, then the chances are that all the bait will have gone by the next day – unless yours was one of the first baits it picked up. Even if it was one of the first baits picked up, you still cannot be sure that more carp will not demolish the bait. The question is, just how much bait do you put out?

The only way that you can effectively be sure that bait is in the swim is to top up on a regular basis. This in itself causes problems. While early season carp do not seem too worried about bait being podded out, the tench seem to take far longer to come into the swim. Once again, the carp get there first.

The 1991–2 season proved a real headache for me. After a three-week campaign for tench I had very little to show in the way of results, with only a few 8lb and lesser fish to my rods. On the other hand, I did extremely well in catching unwanted carp, landing three 20lb ones and a number of good doubles. The water I was fishing is relatively clear at the start of the season, and I had one rod close in to the bank

The author with a brace of 8lb tench.

where some bushes overhung the edge of a channel between two bars, and the other at a range of 40yd. Most of the carp came to the near rod, along with the better tench. The problem I had was that although the tench (including two fish that were easily into double figures) were often in the swim, the carp would come in and push them out. At times, up to five carp came in together and ate the lot. I have since decided that I will fish another water where the carp are very low in density, in the hope that I get better results.

Tench fishing in the Wessex area is beginning to catch up with other areas of Britain. Although no 10lb fish have been caught in the area at the time of writing (apart from at one exclusive and expensive gravel pit in the vicinity of Ringwood), certain pits do contain fish into double figures. The best fish out in the 1991–2 season was 9lb 14½oz, along with a number of back-up 9lb and big 8lb fish – not too far away from the magic 10lb mark! I would think that at least one (if not a few) fish over this weight will be caught in the near future. To this end, a baiting campaign somewhere around four weeks before the start of the season should ensure that the tench know where to find their food. I do not profess to be anywhere near as proficient in the pursuit of tench as anyone who has fished extensively over the years for this species, but I will outline the methods that I now use.

My latest baiting campaign consisted of around 1 gallon of hemp laced with maples and 100 boilies, which I introduced every two or three days. The area that I chose was at a point where there is a drop-off some 30yd or so from the bank of a lake. This drop-off is a gradual shelf that extends for about 3yd, levels out for a further 5yd and then rises sharply up to a fairly large plateau. I could see tench rolling on the top of this plateau and along the contours of the drop-off. There are quite a few bars and features of a similar nature in this pit and the tench generally seem to patrol these in typical fashion from first light onward, announcing their presence by rolling on the surface.

After such a baiting campaign, hair-rigged boilies (now considered the best early-season method) should be fished – one on the bottom and the other lying at an inch above the bottom over the bed of hemp.

Mark holds a 9lb 2 ½oz fish

Once fish start to show, both rods should be switched on to the most productive method, changing around again as bites slow down. As the day goes on, I have found that baits fished well off the bottom seem to catch the odd tench which can be seen cruising around. I really cannot understand why a tench which is primarily a bottom feeder should take a boilie suspended 3ft from the bottom. It has got to be the most unnatural presentation that is possible, but it does catch fish. I took my second-best tench at 8lb 7oz using this method in the middle of the day. My best, by the way, is an impressive 3oz above this, and was taken hard on the bottom.

The hook lengths between bait and lead seem to work better when in excess of 2ft. Shorter hook lengths do produce some blistering runs, but often these do not make proper contact with the fish. Perhaps the way that tench pick up the bait has something to do with this, but I am not sure. As with the majority of my fishing, my hook length material is Kryston. The weight of the lead I use is from around ¾oz, with hook sizes from size 6 down to size 10. Generally, I start off on size 6 Richie McDonald carp hooks made by Partridge, and then reduce the size if I feel that it is necessary. The actual boilie itself is 16mm or less in size, and is fished tight to the bend.The boilies you use should be softer than those used by carp anglers – after all, carp anglers boil the baits until hard to deter tench, so quite the opposite is needed when tench fishing.

As for mixes and flavours, I use baits that have been already prepared by Specialist Bait Supplies. I rarely use boilies for species other than tench, and find that the range offered by this company is more than suitable for my needs. Sweet flavours (such as their excellent strawberry jam used with the dairy mix) or the fishmeal mix seem to work well, as does the High Energy Big Fish Mix. I have also found that the Barbel Mix with Attract Natural is very effective, so much so that on the pit from which my best tench came I seemed to catch a lot of fish from several different swims while those around me struggled. They soon switched over to this bait and had good results for a while, but the sport then tailed right off – even when a new flavour was used. This was probably due to the fact that Barbel Mix has a very low protein value, but as I am no expert on the reasons why a boilie works or not, I will leave this subject well alone. One thing that is certain, however, is that as the season goes on tench do become wary of boilies, and I am sure that the problems involved in maintaining a decent return for effort becomes that much harder.

One consideration in the bait problem issue has recently been brought to my attention. An angler who conducts research into bait

Just 3oz under the 10lb mark!

has produced some very interesting results from experiments on carp that are held captive in a very large tank. In this tank there are four mirrors and two commons. Four of the carp will eat any bait, whether it be boilies, sweetcorn or anything that is carrying a sweet flavour, but the other two will not come anywhere near sweet bait. However, once a savoury bait is introduced these two fish will be on it immediately, while two of the others will take it only occasionally. So here we have two fish that do not mind what they take, two that show a preference for a sweet bait and two that will only take a savoury bait (these two will actually even avoid the area of the tank where the sweet baits are).

The fish were introduced to the tank at weight of up to ½lb, so it would seem unlikely that they had learned to reject a flavour because they had been caught on it. It therefore stands to reason that some fish respond only to a particular type of flavour. With this in mind, if you restrict yourself to only one bait when fishing you will never catch some of the fish at all. The research applies to carp in this instance, but I am sure that is must apply to other species, and tench in particular.

Because my interest in tench stops once they have spawned, I do not have to worry too much about these problems. No doubt anglers who fish for these species longer than I do have their own solutions to the problems, but as far as I am concerned, so long as the bait I am using catches fish and is a decent bait then I do not care which mix, flavour or protein value it has. The very fact that these days I only fish for big fish dictates that once spawned, the tench no longer holds much interest for me. In the past, however, I have caught tench in the winter in conditions far from those that are conventionally considered favourable and whilst intent on other species. Indeed, I have taken tench in gravel pits in sub-zero conditions when using maggots and feeder tactics.

The best method for feeder fishing has got to be the fixed paternoster. Using a Drennan ring as the basis of the rig, with a tail of around 2ft or more and the link to the feeder kept to around 6in, very few tangles result. Bites on this rig are usually sail-away affairs. I still use bait runners in these winter conditions, but drop the line strength to 4lb as weed growth is a lot less than it is in the earlier part of the season. I was tempted to say here that it is non-existent, but what with the warmer winters that we have been having over the last few years, weed never seems to die back completely as it once did. Back-end tench can now be expected to top 8lb, and I must confess that I could easily spend a weekend or two after fish of this calibre.

The capture of fish at this time of year will also give an indication of what to expect the following season, as you can expect approximately a 20 per cent increase in weight of spawn if there is the cold spring that tench anglers hope for. With this in mind, it is well worth making a trip or two to some waters that are less well known with a view to the next year's season should sizeable fish turn up. One other thing, when fishing maggot and feeder I have not found it necessary to use heavy gauge hooks. In fact, finer hooks such as the Drennan Specialist are more than adequate, offering far better presentation and therefore securing more bites and more fish.

River Tench Fishing

This is an avenue that has not yet been explored by many. Both the River Avon and River Stour have more than their fair share of tench, and while most of these are of an average size I do know of a few fish over 8lb from the middle and upper reaches of the Stour. There is no way that I will name the stretch in which they live as I know that a couple of anglers are fishing for the tench on the river in the firm belief that double-figure fish are present. This belief is backed by the fact that the 8lb fish caught so far have all been fully spawned-out fish! The section that these fish are in is deep and slow, relatively underfished and extremely hard going. In the early 1980s I fished for the tench myself, but with only very limited success. In fact, I only caught three fish, the best of which was only slightly over 4lb.

The Avon seems to be a fair bet for a decent tench, as in recent years a number of them have been taken up to around the 5lb mark. These have mostly been winter tench which were caught by roach anglers who were fishing the slacks when the river has been in flood. During the summer months I have observed tench in both of these rivers and in most of the stretches that I fish. Occasionally, I have caught the odd fish by stalking and using sweetcorn for bait when the barbel I usually look for did not show. Once again, I am talking about opportunist fishing here. The places in which tench appear are often not those you would expect, and sometimes they can even be seen in the fastest of runs.

I am reasonably sure that the Wessex rivers are capable of producing a fish into double figures, and wait with anticipation for the first one. I suppose that this section on tench should have been a lot longer than it is, but as my experience of the species has to date been a short-lived affair I have but a limited knowledge on the subject.

A superb 7lb 7oz fish for Dave Tissington.

Zander

The hysteria that this name promotes is well documented in various books of the species. In an ideal world I would like to see this fine predator introduced to the Wessex area, but the likelihood of this ever happening is, to say the least, remote. There are various enclosed pits in the area that are completely overrun with small, stunted fish that would make ideal food for the zander, and the latter would provide a welcome addition. There is actually really only one reason why I am for the introduction of zander, and this is purely selfish. I have recently become involved with the species, but as the nearest viable waters to my house (discounting Bury Hill Lake) are over 200 miles away, the cost of getting to them is rather prohibitive. In theory, their introduction is fine, but in practice I would not welcome any stockings to the Wessex area for one main reason. This is that I believe that some amongst our ranks would soon move stocks to other stillwaters and inevitably, eventually they would make their way into the river systems. As a result, I will have to continue the trek north in an attempt to catch zander.

My very limited experience with zander has been most rewarding so far, and I now have a new personal best to beat – a beautifully marked fish of 1lb 14oz (well, everyone has to start somewhere!). I also had a bonus when fishing the Fens in that I was privileged to see some fine specimen fish.

My first trip saw Mark Vials nearing his personal best with a couple of 9lb fish, as well as a few others for good measure. I became chief camera man on this occasion, and hardly got any sleep as it seemed that every time I nodded off, Mark would appear and ask me to take yet another shot for him. While I was there I also had the pleasure of meeting some of the 'Z' men (this is the name that they affectionately attribute to the zander). My own personal experience of the zander on that occasion was, however, most frustrating. I must have hooked at least half a dozen fish, including one or two quite large ones, only to lose most. As I had a day's fishing already arranged during the last week of the season, the session was split into two halves.

On the second visit Mark and I met up with Kevin Maxfield as arranged. The intended venue was crowded as Mark's success on the previous visit was by then common knowledge. As the weather was also rather hostile, I was in no mood to fish on the middle level for the whole of the remaining season, wanting instead to catch some fish.

After some debate we decided to spend a night or two on the Cut Off. We strung ourselves out about 70yd apart, set the tackle up and then started to prepare dinner. Some time after we had eaten, Mark had a take on the far bank. It was obvious that this fish was large from the start, and when it broke surface it became apparent that it might well be a double. Once it was landed, Mark weighed the fish and it went to 10lb ½oz. Not happy with this and wanting to be absolutely sure that it was a double, Mark asked me the weigh the fish on my scales. I came up with the same result. It was a well-deserved first double after a considerable amount of time and effort.

We then got on with the job of photographing the fish, and as three cameras were involved which were all operated by competent people you would think that the odds of getting it wrong must be very high. So did we! My own camera, until then always reliable in my hands, for some reason managed to overexpose every shot despite the fact that the flashgun is of the same make as the camera and sets the aperture and exposure automatically. Meanwhile, Mark had set his flashgun to the right ASA, but forgot to alter the shutter speed. Fortunately, I pressed the shutter a couple of times before the flash had fully charged – in fact, these were the only shots that came out at all. His other shots consisted of half the picture being in perfect exposure and in focus, while the other half was black. At the same time, Kevin had neglected to make sure that the film in his camera was fully engaged on the spool before closing the back of the camera. This only became evident the following day, although obviously the other faults were not detected until after developing.

Anyway, during the course of the night Kevin had a run on the far bank rod. The first we knew of the fish was when he shouted down the bank in the darkness that he had got one. Mark and I walked up the bank to see the fish, and were greeted by the sight of an immense 'Z'. After the unhooking was completed, various estimations were voiced at around 11–12lb, and when on the scales it proved to be 11lb 5oz. We decided to wait for first light to take the photographs and so Kevin sacked the fish. Shortly before dawn I managed to hook and lose what felt like a good fish once again.

When first light arrived, the camera gear was sorted out once again and we proceeded to take some shots. My camera performed perfectly with the flash on this occasion, and I was then given the job of doing the honours with Kevin's camera. The motor drive appeared to be a lot quicker than mine even though they were the same make, and I noted that there were only two shots left at this point. Five shots later,

Kevin Maxfield with 11lb 5oz of beautiful zander.

I asked Kevin if there was any film in the camera, and as he assured me there was I assumed that either it was not loaded correctly or that it had come out of the canister when it reached the end. It later came to light that it was the former, as when the film was developed Kevin had a whole reel of perfectly black shots. This was completely disastrous, as apart from this fish there would have been another double on this film plus some other good catches. Talk about a load of amateurs!

Anyway, that is the sum total of my involvement with the infamous zander to date. Well, not quite as I did catch one more on the second trip from a section that I have been informed is one of the hardest stretches on the middle level. In fact, both my 'Zs' came from this stretch, and as the other half-dozen 'Z' men failed to catch on this venue at all, perhaps there is hope for me yet!

10

What Next?

With my love for fishing and the waters on which I pursue my sport being of far more importance to me than a regular nine-to-five job, when the opportunity arose to leave what to me was meaningless employment, I took it. I am now able to put far more into the sport then I ever have done before. Fishing has now become a way of life.

From among the many ways that you can earn a reasonable living through angling, an idea came to mind and one that would benefit both myself and, far more importantly, others. Others, that is, who would like to gain first-hand information on how to catch larger-than-average fish consistently, or on how to achieve that fish of a lifetime. The idea was to offer anglers the opportunity to spend a day on the river under my guidance, locating and catching the fish that the rivers in the area hold. Anglers that come to the Wessex area to catch these fish often spend a lot of time and effort just trying to get to grips with the rivers.

The amount of fish reported in the weekly angling papers give a false impression of the Avon and Stour, so that it appears to anglers who have never set eyes on the river that all one has to do is to cast a line into the water and specimen fish appear from nowhere. This is, in fact, nowhere near the truth. Although the rivers do hold more specimen fish of all kinds than any others in the country, these fish do not give themselves up easily, and those anglers who do catch good fish consistently have a very good understanding of the rivers and their constantly changing moods. They also spend far more time on the rivers than any others.

As an experienced Wessex angler I feel that I am in a position to introduce the newcomer to the area or guide in the art of specimen fishing – not so much in how to break a record, but in the aspects of actually making his or her efforts worthwhile. After all, if a visiting angler does not know how to deal with the river then the chances of success are slim. To this end, I will be offering my services as a tutor-come-guide-ghillie and will explain the methods that will lead to success. Each day I spend in this role will be devoted totally to the angler's needs, and the knowledge that he or she gains will prove invaluable in the quest for a dream fish. Who knows, perhaps my pupil will even catch one of those fish on the day. If there is any chance of landing a good fish on the day, then it will happen. Armed with the necessary knowledge, anglers who have spent a day with me will then be able to go out and continue to enjoy consistent success in the future, and by applying the same theories and practices to their home waters, they may well be surprised at what they can offer.

Any anglers who are interested in joining me on the bank for a day or two are invited to telephone me direct on 0836 596341 for further information.

Now on to a final moan!

I have, at times, despaired – as you may have gathered from much of the text in this book – with the different factions of anglers who are constantly at each other's throats. I think it is about time that we all respected each other's chosen ways and stopped bickering amongst ourselves. In angling there is no difference between the specialist, match, game and pure pleasure anglers – in fact, we all fish for pleasure! We do, however, share the same main enemy out there and it is one that will ultimately affect us all – pollution!

We should be fighting together against this enemy and any other aspects that will directly affect our sport, and not fighting each other. Let us learn to accept that some of us do things differently from others and leave each to his own. Do not interfere with one man's sport, because he may well feel the need to interfere with yours.

Stand up and be counted as a body, for as such no one may touch us. As the saying goes: united we stand, divided we fall. Just think about this the next time you consider a rule change at any AGM.

Last but not least, get back out there and catch some fish!

The final word. *Fin*. (Thanks Dave).

11

Useful Addresses

The first body I have listed is one that I believe we should all subscribe to before we can even consider ourselves worthy of bearing the title of angler:

The Anglers' Co-operative
   Association
23 Castlegate
Grantham
Lincolnshire
NG31 6SW
Tel: 0476 61008

For those interested in joining angling clubs which control Wessex rivers:

Mr K. Grozier
Permit Secretary
Ringwood and District Anglers'
   Association
15 Greenfinch Walk
Hightown
Ringwood
Hampshire
Tel: (0425) 471466

Mr B. Heap
Treasurer and Permits
Wimborne and District Angling
   Club

76 Higher Blandford Road
Broadstone
Bournemouth
Dorset
Tel: (0202) 698696

Mr C. Bungay
Chairman and Permits
Christchurch Angling Club
8 Purewell
Christchurch
Dorset
BH23 1EP
Tel: (0202) 474924

For those interested in day tickets:

Ringwood Tackle
5 The Bridges
Ringwood
Hampshire
BH24 1EA
Tel: (0425) 475155
(Tickets for CAC, Ringwood Fishery and The Severals, plus Hurst Pond Hightown and Somerly Lakes Stillwaters.)

Davis Tackle
75 Bargates
Christchurch
Dorset
BH23 1QE
Tel: (0202) 485169
(Tickets for Royalty, Winkton,
CAC and Sopley.)

For those interested in eels:

Mr M. Bowles
Secretary
British Eel Anglers' Club
64 Granville Road
Gillingham
Kent
ME7 2PB